Kind And True

by

Joanna P. Moore

First Fruits Press
Wilmore,
Kentucky
c2018

Kind and true.
By Joanna P. Moore.

First Fruits Press, © 2018

ISBN: 9781621717898 (print), 9781621717904 (digital), 9781621717911
(kindle)

Digital version at
http://place.asburyseminary.edu/firstfruitsheritagematerial/150

For all other uses, contact:

First Fruits Press
B.L. Fisher Library
Asbury Theological Seminary
204 N. Lexington Ave.
Wilmore, KY 40390
http://place.asburyseminary.edu/firstfruits

Moore, Joanna P., 1832-1915
    Kind and true / by Joanna P. Moore. – Wilmore, KY : First Fruits Press,
    ©2018.
        pages 152; 1 cm.
        Reprint. Previously published: Chicago : Fleming H. Revell, c1896.
        ISBN: 9781621717898 (pbk.)

        1. Christian youth--Conduct of life. 2. Courtship--Religious aspects--
        Christianity. 3. Marriage--Religious aspects--Christianity.   I. Title.
    BV4531.M59 2018   241

Cover design by Jon Ramsay

asburyseminary.edu
800.2ASBURY
204 North Lexington Avenue
Wilmore, Kentucky 40390

First Fruits
THE ACADEMIC OPEN PRESS OF ASBURY SEMINARY

First Fruits Press
The Academic Open Press of Asbury Theological Seminary
204 N. Lexington Ave., Wilmore, KY 40390
859-858-2236
first.fruits@asburyseminary.edu
asbury.to/firstfruits

THE AUTHOR AT SEVENTY.

KIND AND TRUE

My Father thou art the guide of my youth. Jer. 3: 4.

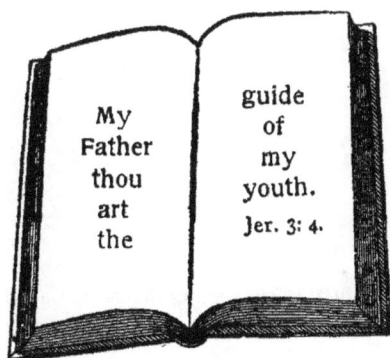

Poverty and shame shall be to him that refuseth instruction: but he that regardeth reproof shall be honored. Prov. 13: 18.

He that walketh with wise men shall be wise; but a companion of fools shall be destroyed. Prov. 13: 20.

Flee also youthful lusts: but follow righteousness, faith, charity, peace, with them that call on the Lord out of a pure heart.—2 Tim. 2: 22.

By Joanna P. Moore.

FLEMING H. REVELL COMPANY,

CHICAGO.   NEW YORK.   TORONTO.

Publishers of Evangelical Literature.

INTRODUCTION

This little book is written for the young to supply a great need, viz.—to give advice and warning along the line of Courtship. Our work for many years has been for the happiness of the Home. We find that the greatest source of domestic discord was a mistake in the selection of a partner for life. And back of this mistake was flirting and courting for fun, as the young people say.

A man or woman who has been addicted to flirting, seldom makes a faithful husband or wife. Perhaps the greatest sin of the age is the levity with which we treat the marriage relation. We joke our boys and girls about their love for the opposite sex, and thus they learn to trifle with the God-given affection that should exist between husband and wife. Our foolish jesting tempts them to tell lies on this subject. Dear young people, Marriage is a very solemn affair; so also is the Courtship that leads up to it. Next to your conversion, your marriage is the most important event of your life. We have wanted the young people to read the Bible with their lovers. To this they objected, because it was not the custom. To make it easy, we have given in this book thirty Bible lessons, part on the subject of Courtship and part on the duties of husband and wife. The text is only referred to, therefore these lessons will gracefully lead to your getting your Bibles and reading from them.

Pray that this little book may help our young people in their pleasant but hazardous selection of the person with whom they must live until death do them part.

PREFACE.

About four years ago I was led by the Spirit to think and pray much for our young people. They are often greatly neglected. We scold them enough, but do we obey the following command? "Fathers, provoke not your children to anger, but bring them up in the nurture and admonition of the Lord." Eph. 6: 4. Nurture means to feed, to protect, to comfort, to encourage, as a nurse would a child. They are surrounded by great temptations, and need our constant care and loving advice and instruction.

Dear Young People: I have talked and prayed for you with your parents for so many years, and helped them plan what was the wisest way to lead you to God. Year by year I have become more and more interested in you, till now I feel as if I loved you almost as much as do your parents. The words of warning and instruction contained in this little book come to you from a loving heart. May God give each one of you a teachable, obedient heart, is my prayer in Jesus' name,

Hopefully in Christ,

SISTER MOORE.

Power and Gladness Through the Holy Spirit.

FOR HOPE, BY REV. C. P. JONES, JACKSON, MISS.

Tune—"He is Just the Same To-day."

Ye shall receive power after that the Holy Ghost is come
upon you.—Acts 1: 8.

Have you learned the precious secret of the Holy Spirit's
power?
Do you know what joy and gladness is your portion every hour?
Do you know that you may always have the Spirit dwell
within?
And that Jesus Christ within you sanctifies and keeps from
sin?

CHORUS.

Oh, be filled, be filled my brother, with the Holy Spirit's power,
Only ask, and God will send Him like an overflowing shower.
Oh, be filled with the Holy Spirit's power.
Oh, my brother, Jesus never meant for you and me to stay
In the flesh, and feebly struggle to obey Him day by day.
In the flesh we cannot please Him nor the works of heaven do,
Jesus Christ has something better than this struggling life for
you.

He has sent the Holy Spirit to fulfil in us the right;
We surrender and receive Him, then He strengthens us with
might.
And the deeds of grace we're doing and the life we thenceforth
live
Is no longer ours; but Jesus through our faith His life doth
give.

Do you find it hard, my brother, to obey the law of love?
Is your heart so cold toward Jesus that your faith you cannot
prove?
Oh, my brother, claim the Spirit, for the promise is to you,
And the *Spirit needs you*, brother, for laborers are few.

What Would Jesus Do?

A young and earnest pilgrim
  Traveling the king's highway,
And conning o'er the lessons
  On the guide-board every day,
Said as each hindrance met him,
  With purpose firm and true,
"If on earth He walked today,
  What would Jesus do?"

It grew to be his watch-word
  In service or in fight;
It helped to keep his pilgrim garb
  Unsullied, pure and white;
For when temptation lured him,
  It nerved him through and through
To ask this simple question,
  "What would Jesus do?"

Now if it is our purpose
  To walk where Christ has led,
To follow in His footsteps
  With ever careful tread,
O let this be our watch-word!
  'Twill help both me and you
To ask in every circumstance,
  "What would Jesus do?"—*Selected*.

CONTENTS.

Young People's Dedication.

Just as I am, young, strong and free,
To be the best that I can be;
For truth and righteousness and Thee
Lord of my life, I come.

In the glad morning of my day
My life to give, my vows to pay,
With no reserve and no delay,
With all my heart, I come.

I would live ever in thy light,
I would work ever for the right,
I would serve Thee with all my might,
Therefore to Thee I come.

—[Selected.]

HELP FOR THE YOUNG PEOPLE.

Several persons have asked me to write something
for those who are under 21 years of age. This will indeed be a great pleasure to talk to the young, but I
will not limit those who listen to twenty=one years,
but we will include all under thirty=five. I am sure
we are young till we are thirty=five. In one sense you
may be young always. I expect you to always keep
a young, hopeful heart. I am sixty=four years old
but my heart is young and glad and hopeful, because
those who have the hope of living with Jesus through
the endless ages of eternity should not let a few years

9

of earth's trials make them feel old. The body may grow old, but the heart should always be fresh and bright with the love of God.

Yet there is one sense in which you are young and I am old. I have traveled many a road and passed safely by many of Satan's traps, besides I have been caught in some of them and had hard work to get out. We that are old have had an experience that will help you to be better men and women than we have been if you will listen to our advice. Let me illustrate:

A farmer was on his way to town to sell a load of wood. He met his neighbor coming home, who said: "Turn back to the cross roads and take the hill road to town, because yesterday I went this road and got into the mud and broke my wagon and lost my load. Oh, I have had a hard time, but I have come back this other way and know it is good." Now the neighbor might have acted stubborn and said, "My team will pull through, I will go ahead," and no one would have pitied him when he lost his load of wood. The good advice would be lost on him. But a wise man would have profited by the experience of his neighbor and taken the best road to town.

I heard a poor father say to his son one day: "John, do not hang around that saloon. When I was young I had no one to teach and help me, therefore I went with bad company till my character was gone, and one night I almost lost my life in a fight. But I have seen the evil of it all. Do, I beseech you, stay at home." But the wicked, ungrateful boy got up and took his hat, and started off, saying, " I will go ahead until I see the evil of it, and you can't stop me." On he went to destruction, and left his parent broken-hearted. But the dear young people who read this will listen to the good advice of older friends, and thereby be able to do more good than we did who had not so many to help us along life's journey.

"Seek First the Kingdom of God."

I have thought of a dozen subjects about which I would like to talk with you—such as music, books, innocent amusements and education in various directions, but every time I was stopped with the sad fact, so few of the young people are Christians, and many more who have made a profession are "lukewarm," and God will spew them out of his mouth, according to Rev. 3: 16, and so they will be lost, and I said to myself, What is the use of fixing them up beautifully for eternal death? Why teach them music? They do not sing in hell! There is "wailing and gnashing of teeth" there, but no songs. In heaven they sing. O yes, glad and glorious is the music there. Why speak of amusements? They may die to-day. In hell there is nothing but pain and suffering, and one in great pain never thinks of any amusement, but only longs to be free from suffering. Why speak of books or education? They are on their way to hell, and in that place of darkness no one could read if they had books, and they may be there before the next school day ends. O how many young people have died this last winter, died without a hope in Jesus. There is only one door to heaven, and that is Jesus. Beloved young people, how I wish I could make you see how true religion would add to all the

enjoyment of life. I do not mean this half-hearted
kind of religion that is never satisfied with God, but
is always running after the world for pleasure. No,
not that kind. There is a kind that bubbles up within your soul, which keeps you fresh and bright and
joyous all day and all night long. After you have
learned how to accept of Jesus as your Savior and
Sanctifier, then we will begin to do all we can from
the human side to polish you up for heaven. We will
get you good books and music and education if we
can, because now you will only want the kind that
will make you shine for Jesus. It will be the only
kind that you can enjoy and the only kind you will
need in heaven. Heaven is a school of education.
We will be constantly learning after we go there, and
what you learn along in the *right* direction on earth
will fit you for a higher class when you enter heaven's
school. O what a grandeur and hopefulness this
gives to all the lessons we learn here.

Now let us settle the question to-day, before you
lay this book down. Do you want to give your young
life to Christ? Do you want to be forgiven? Are
you real sorry for your past sins? If so, I will tell
you how to be saved. Acts 16: 30, 31 tells us to " believe on the Lord Jesus Christ and thou shalt be
saved." Trust Jesus with your whole heart and life.
Heb. 8: 12 says God will forgive our sins and remember them no more. O how glad I am that God forgets my past sins. Phil. 4: 13 tells how you can live a
good life after you are forgiven. " I can do all things
through Christ. " Christ will be with you and keep
you to the end. He loves you; only trust and obey,
and you are safe. May God bless this little Bible

lesson to the saving of my dear young people for Jesus' sake, amen.

Two Prayers for the Young.

I have two great prayers in my heart for the young. First that they may each have a happy home that they *own*—a pure home, a home where jealousy cannot come—a home where there is a wife, "the heart of whose husband doth safely trust in her," Prov. 31: 11, because she is true to him, and where there is a husband "that praiseth his wife," Prov. 31: 28. How sad it is to think that so few husbands know how to praise their wives. Homes are needed where husband and wife have perfect confidence in each other, where they honor and respect the advice of each other, where they always treat each other with respect and politeness. Second prayer is that your happy home may not make you selfish, but that it may lead you to carry the light and love from your fireside to the hearts and homes of those who know not the blessedness that you possess. You must do this for self-protection, if not from love to Christ. No one is independent of their neighbor's home. If the small-pox was next door to you, you could not feel safe, but that disease would only harm the body. The bad influence of wicked neighbors may destroy the happiness of your own beloved home and lead your children astray. The greatest safeguard against this evil influence is *your effort to save and bless them.* Always be busy with some plan to help all within your influence. But you ask, Why do you talk to us about what we are to do when we are married? I am glad you have asked that question, and this is my answer: I want you to *begin* right. It may be too late after you are married six weeks to tell you never to have your *first* quarrel, because often before one week of the honeymoon is over you may have shown some disrepect or lack of confidence in each other that will destroy the happiness of your whole married life. Oh, I do dread the *first* quarrel between husband and wife. It opens the door for the second and third and so on to a life of misery. Now I will put the sum of my prayers into two sentences.

First, that you may have a happy home on earth, and a glorious one in heaven.

Second, that you may do all in your power to make other homes happy. Cannot all young friends say "amen" to these prayers? I want all young people who are courting to be sure to read your Bible with your lover and pray together. I will give you a few texts, and you can hunt up others. Eph. 5: 22–33; Col. 3: 18, 19; Eph. 4: 32: Matt. 6: 14, 15; 1 Tim. 3: 11, 12; Titus second chapter. The rest are all in Proverbs. Prov. 12: 4–11; 11: 22; 24: 30–34; 21: 9–19; 23: 20, 21; 15: 17; 1: 16; 8: 16–19: 31: 10–31.

Hunting for a Husband.

"Yes, that is what I am doing, hunting for a husband," said a young lady not long since. I admired her for her honesty, for that is just what all the young women are doing; the only difference is this: some do it in a very indirect way; some in a very sensible way; some in a very silly way. Well, that matter being settled, I want to tell you the *way to get a good husband,* because the young men are all look-ing for wives, just the same as you are looking for husbands. Two folks hunting, each for the other, are soon found, and that is the reason we have so many weddings. Well, I said I wanted to tell you girls how to get a good husband.

First. *Deserve a good husband;* behave in the gentle lady-like way that any sensible man will ad-mire, and he will be attracted towards you. But if you behave in a foolish giggling way, then some fool-ish fop will like you. As the old saying goes " Birds of a feather flock together." A good young man is looking out for a good wife, one that will help him to build a happy home and make a peaceful fireside, where he can sweetly rest, when the day's work is done: one that can give him sympathy and comfort: one that can be to him a real helpmeet, the proper help just as God intended she should be. If he sees you fond of dress and show, then he will turn away saying, "That woman would keep me poor buying ribbons and ruffles; I should never be able to save money to buy a home in my life if I had her. She would spend half her time before the glass and no time left to get my dinner or cultivate her mind." Again, if he sees that you are forward and bold, talk-ing to all the boys in a saucy, familiar way, trying to get every one to admire and flatter you—now, a man of common sense will leave such a girl. He will say: " Before we are married five months, she will be set-ting traps to catch some other woman's husband. I do not want such a wife."

Again the girl may not be bold, and yet in a sly way be flirting with two or three boys at once: One beau walks with her to and from church; another is her gallant to a party, and a third comes and spends the evening with her. Our sensible young man will shake his head and say: "That girl has too many beaux to suit me; she either has no mind of her own and does not know whom she loves, or else she is wicked and wants to deceive these young men and make them believe she loves them when she does not. I do not want her; she would not be satisfied with the earnest love of *one good man*. I doubt if she knows what true love is," and so he turns away in disgust.

Now, of course, this flirting young girl will marry some silly foolish man like herself, and two fools together will be sure to fight and sue for a divorce before they are married two years. No good young woman will allow even two young men to pay attention to her in the way of a lover at the same time. Be true in your courtship or you will not make a true wife.

Again, if our sensible young man comes to your home and finds it all in disorder—he *may* come some time when you are not expecting him, and find you dirty and ragged. Then he will say to himself, "That is the way she will look after she is married." So he turns away with a shudder. Young girls, *always* keep yourself neat and nice, even at your work. You *can* do it; you ought to do it. Every man likes a neat good housekeeper. Many a man has been driven to the saloon or grocery to spend his evenings just because his home was all dirty and in disorder. Now, girls, if you want a good husband, keep your person and your house neat, clean and in order.

*At home be always neat and nice,
  Though no one may admire,
And do not go about the house
  In slovenly attire.
With slipshod shoes, ungartered hose
And rag tag skirts and furbelow
With hair uncombed and dress unloosed."

Again, if a thoughtful good young man hears you speak in a cross disrespectful way to your father and mother, he will say: "I do not want her; a woman that does not respect and love her parents will not respect and love her husband."

Now, girls, do not forget what I say. Be modest, quiet, intelligent, industrious; stay at home and mind your work, and that sensible young man will find you some day, that is, if you are not in too big a hurry to get married. A good man is worth waiting for. *No* husband is better than a *bad* one.

We have not told the young men how to find a good wife, but they are quick to take the hint. They will know how after reading this article to the girls.

The Kind of a Wife I Need.

We believe in marriage. We hope every young man may find a woman who will satisfy his heart, who will be the joy and inspiration of his life, one whom he can love well enough to die for her if need be, one that will be a helpmeet in all the duties of life, one that will be a wise counselor in his business transactions, one with whom he can read and study to the advantage of both. But especially does he need a wife that can help him in the study of the Bible and in the worship of his God.

I want him to have a wife so dear that he will see that it is impossible for him to seek enjoyment without wanting his beloved by his side. A wife that is able to weave herself into her husband's business, his study, his recreation, and his days of sorrow and trouble, one that understands his weak places and can show him how to make them strong, one that understands his strong points and can direct them into right channels; yes, one that can help develop all that is good and noble in her husband's heart and brain, and with a woman's matchless tact correct his faults, surely such a wife would be a blessing from the Lord. Any man is rich who has such a wife, and let me tell you there are such wives and not a few of them.

Young man, will you try to prepare yourself for such a gift from the Lord?

"Houses and riches are the inheritance of fathers, but a *prudent* wife is from the Lord." Prov. 19:14.

It will be a sad day for the dear wife if she ever finds you are a worthless deceiver. It is true that

"Woman's love, like ivy,
    Too often clings around a worthless thing."

My dear boy, you must try to be as *good* and as *pure* and as *honorable* as the girl you are seeking to win for a wife.

But, young man, be honest; is the above description your ideal of a wife or had you only thought of a wife as being a person who would cook your dinners, mend your clothes, keep your house in order, and attend to your business, and milk the cows and feed the pigs and do the drudgery around your house, in other words be your servant and gratify all your de-

sires even down to the lowest part of your nature?
Yes, be honest. This is exactly the idea *some* men
have of a wife's duty. Well, my boy, until you have
a better and nobler conception of a wife's duty we
hope you will never get one. I know some men who
are very willing to let the wife work and support the
family while they loaf around the streets or saloons,
Many a woman is to-day making her full hand on the
farm, in the cotton patch, and while her *husband rests*
she cooks, cleans the house and takes care of her children to the best of her ability. What do you think
of such a man? Could a good woman cover up all
his faults? I have seen her try very hard to do so.

May God shelter our dear young girls from such
husbands.

You need a wife who knows how to cook healthy
food for her family and make and mend garments,
one who will keep her home neat and in order. O
yes, a good wife " worketh willingly with her hands."
Read Prov. 31:10–31. It describes a good wife, study
it carefully.

The Kind of a Husband I Need.

I am sure there riseth up in the heart of every true
woman a picture of a devoted husband, a happy home
and little loving hands clasped in hers as she kneels
in prayer. God grant that you may realize your
dream of a true Christian home, where you will be
queen.

Now about the kind of a husband that you need:
one that you can *respect* and *honor.* Girls often tell
me that the *first* thing is *love,* but I tell them nay, I

am not going to give my heart away till I am sure I have a safe, honorable and respectable place in which to deposit it. Girls, let me tell you, your heart is the most valuable part of you. Please do not part with it till you are sure you *have one as good in return.* I have no sympathy with girls who stand ready to love any silly fop with a cane and cravat; do it before they have studied his character. You must *not love* till you find something *lovable to love.* How can you love a drunkard or a glutton, one who is always talking about his stomach and something nice to eat, or he may be a licentious man who loves to gratify lust, or perhaps he is lazy and will gladly lie in bed while you cut the wood and make the fires. Perhaps he is an ignorant man, one who does not care for books, not even the Bible. I know an intelligent woman who married a man who could not read, thinking she could teach him, but after marriage he would not be taught. Therefore she must go through life carrying the weight of this ignorant husband. However, I do know some men who are glad to be taught by the wife and have thereby become intelligent. I have known hundreds of wives who have learned how to read after marriage. Our Fireside School is doing a great work in this direction. I know kind, good husbands who cannot read and yet make an intelligent wife very happy, but this is the exception.

Remember the wife must reverence the husband. Eph. 5:33. It will be a moral impossibility for you to "reverence" a man that is not pure and honorable and manly. It must be one to whom you can "look up," not one upon whom you must look down upon with contempt. You want a husband that will be very tender and thoughtful about caring for you when sick, one who tries to shelter you from the hard, coarse things of this life, and yet one that has such an appreciation of your wisdom that he will come to you for advice and sympathy on all occasions. You want a husband that understands that marriage is a partnership affair, that he must consult his wife about his business and all his plans for making a living and educating his family. In fact, husband and wife should advise with each other about all the little details of life; only in this way can they secure perfect unity and harmony in all that pertains to home. A good wife is a companion, not a servant, and a good husband treats his wife as such, and recognizes the fact that she has an *equal right to all the money* that is earned. She does not need to beg her husband for money for the household, or for anything else. Of course, I am talking to a prudent wife, who will not be extravagant. But, perhaps, it is as great a sin to be stingy as to be extravagant. God's cause must be cared for. A gift from the husband is also a gift from the wife, and *visa versa*. Perhaps you had better talk this matter over with your lover and see if he agrees with you.

But, dear girls, never marry a man because you want him to take care of you. You are a strong, brave woman, and you will really, in one sense, take as much care of your husband as he does of you. You are mutually helpful.

I have heard so many women say, " I was poor and married so that I might have some one to work for me." Yet after marriage she did more than her share in supporting the family. You marry because you want to build a beautiful Christian home and be a blessing and help to your husband, because you can earn your own food and raiment, and you *will do it* after you are married. You will keep the home in neat order; perhaps you can make your and your husband's clothing, and it may be, occasionally earn a dollar or two, but no good husband will wish you to do this, if thereby you neglect home duties. Of course, your lover will be very willing to promise this now, but look straight into his eyes and down into his heart and see if he has the true manliness that will insure the promise kept. But, dear girls, last of all, and best of all, your husband *must be a Christian if you are one yourself*, so that you may have sympathy and companionship along on that higher part of your nature. You will go through life with a longing hunger in your soul, if you do not have a husband with whom you can enjoy your religion. It will be just as sad and lonely for the Christian husband who has a worldly wife.

The Use of Courtship.

In Christian lands this is a subject of great interest to young people. In most of the heathen lands the wife is engaged to the husband when she is a baby or a very little girl. This is usually done by the parents so that neither the man nor the woman has anything to do with selecting a partner for life; but in our and other Christian lands we select the man or woman who is to be our partner for life. The object of courtship is to see if the young man or woman is the right one to marry; before they marry they want to know each other, get acquainted with each other's disposition and temper and tastes. Of course, to find this out they must spend some time in what we call court-ship.

A young woman over there asks " How will I know when my friendship for a young man has ended in courtship?" You may talk with a young man or walk with him occasionally, as you would with any friend, or he may come to your home because he is your brother's friend or the friend of the family, but when a young man comes especially to see you that is courtship. When he wants to see you alone then he is a lover, and if you want to see him alone then you have some remote idea at least of selecting each other for husband and wife. You may not admit it to your-self but it is there unless you are a flirt and want to deceive the young man.

Now, my dear young lady, we will give you a few general rules for this important business. Yes, busi-ness, and you must mean business and not fun when you begin. Notice carefully the conduct and words of this young man. If he puts his hands on your per-son in a very familiar way as if he could take any liberty he chose, show him in a quiet, dignified way that this will not do. Take notice if the young man admires you because you are respectful and obedient to your parents and pleasant to your brothers and sis-ters. Does he seem to appreciate the good and sweet things about your character, when you try to help others and wear a smile even when unpleasant things happen; is he interested in finding out how intelli-gent you are, how much you know? These are the good things about you that will last after your young face is withered and old.

It is by these virtues of the heart and mind and soul that you will be able to keep fresh the love of your husband through the days of sickness and trouble. Does he love you for your meek and gentle spirit, for the heart and brain that you have? But suppose the young man does not seem to care much about these but he simply wants to spend the evening in hugging and kissing you and in saying silly flattering words, how sweet you are and how much he loves you, then that young man's love is too sensual. It is not pure enough. How many young people sit up courting, as they say, till 1 o'clock at night, and not one sensible word have they spoken; I remember asking a young girl some questions about her lover with whom she had spent several evenings and was about to marry him. The questions as I remember were these:

"Can the young man read?"

"I do not know?"

"Is he a Christian?"

"I don't know!"

"How does he think the Sabbath ought to be spent in a home?"

"I never asked him!"

"Has he any money to fix up a home?"

"I never asked him, I do not know."

"Does he think it is best for you to stay with your mother after you are married?"

"We never talked about what we would do after we were married."

I saw these two people together. Even in company she would lean up close to him and he would hold her hand in his and sometimes put his arms around her.

Shame, shame, girls.   Sit at a respectful distance from
your lover, look him in the eye to see if he is in earnest, talk to him on sensible subjects.

Courtship is a very important affair.   Keep your
eyes open.   This is your only chance that you will
have to find out the real character of your lover.   He
has a better chance, my sister, to know you than you
have him, because he comes to your home.   If you
could go to his home also it would be a nice arrangement.   Then you would see how he treats his father
and mother.

Tell your lover your idea of what a home ought to
be, and ask his opinion.   Find out if he is saving of
his money.   If he is kind to his sisters and mother,
or if he is selfish.   Keep your mind awake, do not let
your feelings run away with your brains.   Kisses and
caresses have a use, a time when they are greatly
needed and that is after marriage.   But many young
people use them all up before they are married and
have none left for after marriage.   Some day your
husband will come home all discouraged and tired
out, some trouble has come to him.   Then, dear wife,
go to him in your most tender and loving way, put
your cheek close to his and tell him how you love
him, how all day you have been thinking of the many
good and kind things he has done for you.   Tell him
that every day he grows more dear to you.   Now is
the time for kisses, ah?   But you say we used them
all those nights we sat up courting.

Some evening the husband comes home and finds
his wife all discouraged.   Everything has gone wrong
during the day.   Now, dear husband, take this sweet,
tired wife on your knee, hold her close to your heart

and tell her she is the best wife in town. Tell her what a comfort she is, and how proud you are of her; say all the loving words that your heart ought to be full of. They will do no harm now. If young people would be careful not to waste all their love before marriage we would have fewer divorces and fewer unhappy marriages, or I should rather say if they would carefully examine the *kind* of *love* they have for each other. Is it a love founded on the real virtues that each possesses. The goodness of the heart, the kindness of the soul and not on youthful lust? The purest, deepest love does not show itself in hugs and kisses. It flows out in self=denial, self=sacrifice for the comfort and happiness of the loved one.

What I have said to the young lady that asked me a question will apply to young men as well as young women.

Good Sense Courtship.

Some young people make courtship a joke, or silly pastime, or, worse still, a medium of falsehood and deceit. A plan by which they win the heart only to ruin the character. Alas, alas, how many lies are told in courtship, how often we try to deceive each other; in actions, at least, show a decided preference for one that at heart we detest. O boys and girls, don't, don't even *act* a lie! Be honest, be truthful; a lie is a lie, if told between lovers all the same as if it were told in a business transaction.

I want to repeat what I said about the foundation of your love, because it is so important for both boys and girls. Take notice if your lover admires you be-

cause of the good and noble traits in your character
Does the young man appreciate your respect and love
for your parents, and your pleasant manners with
your brothers and sisters, your self-control, your ability to bear unkindness with a loving spirit? Is he
interested in finding how intelligent you are; how
patient, how helpful? Because, my dear child, these
are the good things about you, that will last long after
your young face is withered and old. It is by these
virtues of the heart and mind and soul that you will
be able to keep fresh the love of your husband
through the days of sickness and trouble, and also by
means of the same noble traits of character will the
husband be able to hold and keep the warm devotion
of his darling wife. But if, instead, your lover admires and praises your beautiful face and elegant
dress, if he wants to spend the evening in hugging
and kissing you, and in saying silly flattering things
about how sweet you are and how much he loves
you; and if *you enjoy* all this foolishness, then your
love is not as pure as it should be.

If the young lady admires you because you wear a
fashionable cravat and gold ring and if she is willing
to have you spend money for her lavishly, this is
to you, young man, a token that she is fond of display
and that she is selfish.

Do not be in too great a hurry to be engaged. Wait
till you know each other. Next to your conversion,
your marriage is the greatest event of your life.

I have one more bit of advice: Tell your mother
about your lover. Mother is the best confident you
can have: she is a far better one than your thoughtless boy and girl companions. Now I fear you will

laugh at this and say, "O pshaw, I am not going to tell mother what I say to the girls and what they say to me," and vice versa. Well, laugh if you will, but be assured your mother, if she is a true mother, is the one that can help you more than any earthly friend. In this, more than any other transaction of life, consult your parents, especially mother.

> "Trust your mother, noble youth,
> Turn not from the path of truth;
> In temptation's evil hour
> Seek her ere it gains new power;
> She will never guide you wrong,
> Faith in her will make you strong."

Courtship is something very sweet, very interesting, and I want you to remember that it should last after marriage. It should grow dearer and better as years go by; yes keep it up in its beauty and purity. But I beseech you, do not court any one but your own wife or husband. Be very careful on this point. Love is jealous. It will not, it cannot, share its love with another. Be polite and respectful to other men and women, but be very sure that your actions toward them do not look the least bit like courtship. I say this now so as to warn the young against receiving attention from married persons.

Dear young men and women, my prayers go with these words. I cannot tell you how deeply I feel what I have said. I do not want you to do wrong along on the line of courtship. "Keep thyself pure," "Flee youthful lusts," are God's commands.

The Use of Understanding What I Need.

We have had a lesson on the kind of a wife a young

man should seek to gain.   Also one for our girls on
the subject, "What kind of a husband should I accept?" This may not look like getting ready for
marriage, but it really is an important preparation.
If I am going to the store to buy a dress, the first
question to settle is, what kind of a dress do I need?
I fix on the price and quality of the article to be purchased.   Then if the storekeeper has what I want, it
will not take long to make the bargain.   But suppose,
instead, that you do not know *what you want*.   Then
the clerk will urge you to buy this and that article.
Soon you are bewildered and you buy something that
you do not want—all because you do not have an intelligent idea about the kind of a dress you needed
or ought to have.   So many articles are purchased,
and so many wives selected, and so many husbands
accepted in this careless, haphazard way.   Alas, alas,
after you have them you find you have been cheated,
but is too late to rue your bargain.   Now about a
dress or houses and lands, it may not make much difference, but your marriage contract lasts till death.
Dear young people, before you begin any love-mak-
ing, find out as nearly as possible the kind of a partner you want to walk hand and hand with you
through life.   Then prepare yourself to be worthy of
you ideal.   This is a good beginning.   Perhaps I can
illustrate.

A young man wanted a wife who would care more for
home than for going abroad.   He saw a young lady
that attracted him.   He invited her to accompany
him to a social gathering.   She accepted, and he
called for her on the appointed evening.   She was
ready, but remarked, "The baby has not been very

well and mother is very busy, and I have almost regretted that I promised to go, because I am needed at home. Excuse me and I will go and see how baby is now." The baby was no worse, and mother urged her to go, because the family did not want to offend the young man. He was respectable and good, and the young lady also admired him more than she wanted to acknowledge even to herself; but there was the tired mother and pile of clothes to be ironed, and baby needed attention. Our dear girl decided she would stay at home, though the mother urged her to go. She went back to her lover and stated in an artless, earnest manner why she chose not to go with him to the party. He excused her and went to the party without her, and as he went he said to himsefl, "This is the article for me. This is the girl for me. She cares more for mother and little brother than she does for a party. I will have her if I can get her." He got her, and is happy to-day. This young man knew what he wanted, and because he had good sense to appreciate her noble self-denial, she concluded he was the boy she wanted.

Criticisms.

Since I wrote the foregoing article on courtship I have had several letters on the subject. Some agree with me, others disagree. One young man says: " If my girl will not accept of my kisses before marriage, I will conclude that she does not love me, and would not value them after marriage." I want to say to the young man, in reply, that such little tokens of affection might be all right if taken in small quantities, as you would put a little spice in your pudding, but a pudding all made of spice would not be good. It would make you sick. The deepest affection is not always shown in the way to which he refers. Self-denial, for the sake of the loved one—willing to restrain your feelings, your passions, to please the one you love—this is a higher test of your affection. Let us come back to the real object of courtship. Is it not that you may ascertain or find out the real character, the real worth of your friend? For example, the young man referred to can show his love or appreciation by noticing and mentioning, in a kindly way some self-denying act of his lover. Perhaps she rises to give her father a chair, or she hastens to the kitchen to relieve her mother of some burden, or she gives up her own plans to oblige her brother. Young man, you may notice these things in a way that will make the dear girl you love think, "If this man were my husband, he would be grateful when I tried to please him. He would notice when I was sick and tired, and he would help me, and not do as I have seen some husbands, sit down to dinner, eat heartily, and never notice that the poor wife ate nothing, but seemed only to care for himself. "Your girl" will be studying you while you are studying her character. In a thousand ways you are striving to find out the character and the ability of each other. Is not this one great object of courtship? Now, tell me, how much will you learn of each other by indulging in these loving caresses, that you enjoy so much. Do just tell me, as you sit there in the dark, what good comes of it? My dear young friends, there is a great deal of what you call *love* that is really *lust*. It is simply self-gratification. We had better learn a little self-control even as regards the ardent demonstration of our real love. Self-control is a great attainment. If some persons see but a stick of candy and *want it*, they will give the last nickle to get it. They have no control over their appetites. Out of such persons it is easy to make drunkards and gluttons and adulterers.

It is the lack of ability to control your feelings that often makes young people marry before they are ready to get married. I know a very good and noble young man who was engaged to his wife five years, during which time they were both true and faithful to each other. The reason they did not marry was this: He wished to complete his course in college, and knew that would take all the money he could earn. He did not wish to marry till he could have a home and take the proper care of his wife and family. *They* could deny themselves the pleasure of being husband and wife, though they loved each other tenderly and devotedly. That was a higher love than the love that the young man had who concluded his girl did not love him because she would not allow him to fondle and kiss her for hours.

Another young man writes the following:

"I have looked carefully over your lecture on marriage where you say 'woman's love, like ivy, too often clings around a worthless thing.' I expect if you looked close into the world you would find that 'man's love, like ivy, too often clings around a worthless thing.' Yes, you may allow the same proportion in both the sexes. Take the girls as they come, and the boys as they come, and they are about ditto. You say, how could a girl love a wicked, dissipated man? Well, I ask, how could a man love a wicked, worthless woman? Again, you say, many a woman marries so she can have some one to take care of her, and then after she is married she has to do more work than ever before. But I tell you many girls do much less work after they are married. You tell what a prudent wife will do. Well, will not a prudent husband do the same? Give them both a fair chance. Ask the prudent boys what they think and do not cast a scorching suspicion on all the boys."

If I understand this young man's letter, he thinks there are as many bad girls as there are boys, and that men are fooled in marriage as often as girls are. He may be right. In one article I told the prudent young men the kind of wives I thought they ought to have, and in another I described the kind of a husband that a prudent girl should select. Is not that giving both a fair chance? I wish that we could get the *right boy* and the *right girl* together in every marriage. I hope every boy and every girl may be thoughtful and careful, and not allow themselves to be fooled in this great transaction of marriage. It may be, as this young man says, that the boy is in as great danger as the girl. I mean in danger of making a mistake in the selection of a partner for life.

The young women, as far as I have heard from them, say they agree with my advice, and most of the young men, also. I am thankful for this last criticism, because it emphasizes the fact that young men are often deceived, which I hope will make them more thoughtful and careful. Young men, keep your eyes open and *do not let* the girls fool you.

Education.

Several of the young people have written, asking

if an education should not come before marriage.
Yes, indeed. The education of heart and head and
hands, but not necessarily a college education. That
is only for the few.

Of course we will keep on learning in all these
directions as long as we live if we are earnest, enter-
prising men and women, but a good and broad
foundation should be laid before marriage. Boys
and girls should have a correct knowledge of the
common English branches in their heads. Their
hearts should be filled with love to God and man and
a good knowledge of the Bible.

A wife's hands should know how to cook healthy
food for her family and make garments for herself
and husband and children. A husband should have
some useful trade, or know how to earn money in some
honest employment, and be able at least to mend a
broken chair and put up a shelf in the kitchen for his
wife.

Wedding Day.

My dear young friends, I am going to repeat some
things I have said, because it is a good thing to review
lessons that we are anxious to remember. O beloved
friends, our greatest need is happy homes, and we will
never get these until the subject of courtship is rightly understood.

O what a rainbow of beauty and love should encir-
cle our wedding day, and all the days of wedded life.
God intended the home should be the sweetest and
brightest spot on earth; but alas, how few happy
homes—noise and strife, angry words, and sometimes

angry blows, have blighted our dearest hopes. Now, these things *ought not so to be.* No one enjoys this unhappiness. If only the poor husband and wife knew how to bring back the sunshine and love, they would do it. But if the love and confidence of married life is once lost it is the *hardest* thing in the world to regain. Dear bride and groom, let me whisper in your ear: " Be *sure and never have the first quarrel;* " if you do, the second one will follow, and the third, and so on. " Watch and pray; " burn your tongue with a hot iron rather than let it speak an unkind word to the loved one by your side. But the real remedy for unhappy homes is farther back. There is not care and prayer enough in the selection of your partner for life. How carelessly we lay the foundation of home. A great deal of silly love talk, a few evenings spent in outward tokens of effections, and then they conclude they are ready to get married. But they have not learned each other's real character. They have no plans for house-keeping. No money to fix up a house. They have no idea of the trials of their love and patience that every-day life will bring. They have not counted the cost. They know nothing of that pure love that finds its greatest happiness in seeking the happiness of its loved one, that love will make it so easy for the wife to obey her husband, because that husband's love is so intense that he is willing to lay down his life for his wife.

Husbands, love your wives even as Christ also loved the Church and *gave Himself for it.* Eph. 5: 25. You see his love is compared to the love of Christ for the Church. With such love, no hard command will be given, no heavy burden will be laid on the wife. But my dear young man, how do you know that you have found a woman that you can love enough to die for her?

What sweet traits of character have you seen, what self-sacrifice has she shown? Have you noticed how she treats her father and mother. Does she spend her money to dress herself and let them go shabby? What care does she take of her little brother and sister? What is she doing to help others? Does she know how to deny herself for the good of others? Is she a good housekeeper? How do you agree as to the subject of religion? Have you prayed together over this subject of marriage? Have you read the Bible together to see what God says on the subject? And now, my dear young woman, let me ask you a few questions.

What do you know about this man into whose hands you give yourself? Remember you promise to honor him, look up to him with respect. Is he noble and manly so that you can honor him? What do you know about his home life? Does he know how to deny himself to make others happy, or is he selfish and does he want the best of everything for himself? Does he want everyone to do just as he says? What will be required at your hands? Remember your promise to obey him. Are you old enough to understand whether you really love him or not? Do stop and pray over it. The wedding day is the most solemn day of your life. The day of your death is nothing compared with it. Your work and your care are all over when you die. But this bargain you make to-day will last till death. There is no honorable way out of it. They tell us there is one way out, but it is not an honorable way, and you do not want to get out that way. Yes, marriage is a glad but a very solemn thing, and yet it is treated as a funny joke, something to laugh about, yes and tell lies about. Perhaps the very day before they are married they will deny they are even going to marry. Is it not strange that we take this purest and sweetest sentiment of earth and treat it with levity all the way through, make it a laughing stock, a funnny joke. I tell you it is wrong, it is a desecration of a sacred thing. In this way the world has learned to trifle with human hearts till all are learning to be false. This is the worm at the root that is eating the beauty and freshness out of our home life. I want thoughtful men and women to stop and think. Are we doing things according to the pattern God has given?

Are Marriage Engagements Binding?

I have had several letters asking questions on the above subject. By marriage engagements we understand the promise of lovers to be joined in wedlock at some future time. Surely of all the promises in the world this should be held the most sacred; surely any one who will trifle with the love of the human heart is a murderer of the worst kind. Yes, murderer, because many a true loving heart has been cursed for life because of misplaced confidence in one they loved. I want to caution our young people against hasty engagements. There is a great deal of bogus love these days; it boils over from shallow hearts when the least heat is applied; it is all froth, there is no substance to it.

John says to Mary, after a very slight acquaintance, perhaps, "Oh, you are the darling of my heart, I cannot live without you; you are the joy of my life; I must have you for my wife," and much more of the same nonsense. Dear foolish Mary drinks it all in and promises to marry him. A few weeks after she hears that John is making love to some other girl, and then again to another. She becomes a little jealous and ventures to ask John if the stories that are going the rounds are true. He is angry and indignant, and declares that they are all false, but somehow Mary is not quite satisfied. There is a fear and unrest in her heart, and also in the heart of John lest he be detected.

Now perfect love casts out fear and gives a restful confidence in each other. This will be the case when you have found the true love that satisfies the heart. Other lovers will have no attraction for that heart. It has found its resting place. But this is not the way with our friends Mary and John. It seems to me that the wisest thing they can do is to honestly say to each other, "We will consider our engagement broken till we can have perfect confidence in each other, and if at some future time the mists are all cleared away we may come together, but now we are each free to choose another companion if we wish." Insist upon being free, and then if they really love they will come together again. Is not this the best way to settle such love quarrels?

No honorable persons will hold another one to an engagement against his or her will in love affairs. But the better way would be not to enter hastily into engagements. Let love have time to quiet itself, and

settle down in the nest God made for it. Yes, wait
on the Lord, and do not be too eager. Do not let
your heart run away with your common sense and
good judgment. Suppose you never marry anyone.
It will not be the greatest calamity that ever hap-
pened to mortal being. We admit that a married life
is the happiest when we are properly mated, but we
must also admit that the greatest misery comes from
unhappy marriages. A mistake in the selection of a
partner will blight your whole life

Dear young friends, if ever you needed God's help
it is on the subjects of courtship, engagement and
marriage. I know the world laughs and makes a
joke of the whole affair, but it is all wrong. Marriage is the foundation of home, and home, a happy
home, is the dearest treasure on earth. This is the
reason we want you to court in a common sense way
and give up your foolish fondling and kisses. You
are too lavish with these; they develop a low kind of
love, a love that will not stand the test of married
life. Study your lover's character, study his or her
every day life as far as you can. Notice how they
treat their parents and brothers and sisters. Are they
industrious and honest in their dealings?

We will tell you one way in which you can know
true love from its counterfeit. True love seeks the
happiness of its loved one. No sacrifice is too great,
it does not seek its own pleasure or gratification, but
tries to please and comfort the beloved; and yet true
love is firm for right and truth. It seeks to please
for good according to Rom. 15: 2.

A woman is just as likely to be selfish as a man.
But true love is not selfish. A woman is often a flirt,

and shows by her actions that she loves the man that she does not love. She tries to win only to cast the loving heart aside, even though it break by her unkindness. Oh, this is very cruel in either man or woman.

To sum it all up, be honest and faithful in your love affairs. Be cautious about making engagements to marry, also a bad engagement is better broken than kept. We do not think that long engagements conduce to happiness. Very young persons had better not make solemn promises of marriage. Perhaps after they are educated or old enough to marry they may not like the choice of early years. They can love each other all the same without promising to marry. There is one other evil that often follows engagements, namely, too much familiarity. They take too much liberty with each other. Be cautious, be reserved until after marriage.

Duties of Husband and Wife.

Mary—"Cousin Jane, what makes you look so serious the very day before you are to be married? It seems to me that you ought to be running over with joy."

Sarah—"Well, dear cousin, I am glad, but there is a little of sorrow in my heart. James is good, I know he loves me, and will make a good husband, but some things that look good do turn out to be sad and sorrowful."

Mary—"Why, what do you mean? Are you afraid that James will prove false to you?"

Sarah—"Oh, no; no, cousin. Do not think of such

a thing. James will be faithful to me. But now, you will not misunderstand me, when I tell you what has cast a shadow over my joy."

Mary—"No, dear, we understand each other, so go.

Sarah—"You remember Carrie Strong, who was married to Will Gordon, about three years ago. Both seemed so good and devoted to each other and lived so happily together for two years, but now they are in great trouble."

Mary—"Oh, I remember them very well. How could Satan have gotten into their dear home?"

Sarah—"All through a little bit of jealousy. Will is away from home much of the time and some mischief maker told him evil tales about his wife. He accused her of unfaithfulness. She denied it. But the door of strife was opened and could not be closed."

Mary—"Oh, deliver us from the tongue of the tale-bearer. How much evil a few thoughtless words may do."

Sarah—"Yes, truly, we all need to pray, 'Oh, Lord, set a watch over my mouth.' Well matters grew worse and worse, and night before last, when Will came home, Carrie had his supper all ready and received him kindly, but he immediately began upbraiding her and she denied. But one word brought on another and finally Will gave his dear wife an awful beating, nearly killed her. Her screams brought the neighbors and they went for the doctor. For a long time they thought her dying, but she is now better."

Mary—"What are they going to do with Will?"

Sarah—"Nothing. A great many think Carrie

was to blame, and the general opinion among so
many is, that a husband has a right to whip his
wife."

Mary—"Oh, horrible! Is that the way people believe in this State? Then I shall never make my
home here."

Sarah—"These are the facts. Most men treat
their wives like children, and require implicit obedi-
ence in all things. They seldom ask the wife's advice about anything. She is the servant, and often
stands and waits on her husband as he eats his meals.
She seldom sits down to eat with him. He insists
that she must obey."

Mary—"Yes, but there are two sides to this bargain. Here is my Bible; let me read you: 'As the
church is subject to Christ, so let the wives be to
their own husbands in everything.' That is the
wife's part of the bargain. Now listen: 'Husbands,
love your wives even as Christ also loved the church
and gave himself for it.' (Eph. 5: 24, 25.) That is
the husband's part. I would gladly agree any day
to obey a man who would love me as Christ loves his
church.

Sarah—"Yes, that is so, cousin. Christ loved His
church enough to die for it—'gave himself for it.'
Then He loves His church when they do wrong. He
is tender and kind and patient with his church.
Much more is required of the the husband than of
the wife, you see."

Mary—"No man that loved his wife as Christ
loves His church would beat her, and scold her. No,
indeed, not even when she was unfaithful to him."

Sarah—"Besides Christ calls His church, friends,

not even servants: He reveals to them His secrets; He takes the church into fellowship with himself, and that is what the Husband ought to do with his wife."

Mary—"But when the husband fails to keep his part of the bargain, what can the poor wife do? How can she continue to love and obey a man that treats her cruelly?"

Sarah—"Well, cousin, you see it is a tremendously solemn thing to get married, for both man and woman. James and I have prayed over it often, and as we clasped each other's hands in this covenant of love, we felt that God's strong, kind arms were around us both: therefore, we have no fears while thus upheld."

Mary—"Yes, my dear sweet cousin, God will keep you and yours safe. Never let a doubt enter. But some other day we will finish this subject and we will pray that the laws of the land *shall punish every husband that beats his wife.*

Be A True Woman.

Aim to be a true woman, stout hearted and brave;
Be one of the brightest of gifts God ever gave.
Be not fashionable, idle or vain,
But a woman to grapple with sorrow and pain.
Be a woman of smiles, not a woman of tears,
Be a woman of hope, not a woman of fears.
Be a woman of joy, when sorrows assail,
Be a help, not a clog, when misfortunes prevail.
Never mind if mistakes your life-path should throng,
Never mind a few jolts, as you journey along.
Be true to yourself, and be true to your God.
Be a home-joy, a solace, the best that you can;
Oh! be what God made you—"a helpmate" to man.
                                        —*Everybody's Magazine.*

"The Girls We Loved Made the Difference."

Tom—Bob, see here, you must come and sit down and let us have a talk about old times.

Bob—I am delighted to see you. We have not met before for seven years, not since we were school boys together. We were about the same age.

Tom—Yes, just one day's difference in our age. Now we are both twenty-three years old, but what troubles me is that you know so much more than I do. Why, Bob, I opened my eyes in wonder when I heard you make that speech last night. I could learn faster than you when we were in school together.

Bob—Yes, nature, or I ought to say God has given you remarkable talents. You ought to have made a smart man. You had more money and more friends than I had. Your parents were willing and able to help you. Mine were not able.

Tom—That is true, that is all true, and here you are a graduate and I have not been in college but one year, and yet I intended to get an education. I do not drink nor smoke. What has been wrong with me, and how did you climb up so high? Do tell me.

Bob—Well, since we were old friends, I will tell you a secret. A girl did it all. Four years ago I was quite discouraged. Mother keeps sick and father is not able to work much, and my brother Harry is a bad boy, always getting into trouble, so I gave up and said, "I will never go to school again. Well, about that time, while I had the blues awful bad, I met a young lady one evening at the house of a friend. Her parents had just moved to that place. She was quiet and modest but thoughtful, and somehow we were friends right away. We did not say so, but we seemed to understand each other from the first. I called at her home and had a talk with her father. He invited me to supper, and I told the whole family how much I wanted an education, but that it was impossible to get it. I glanced over at Mary, for that is my girl's name. Her face was full of pity and interest, and into my soul came a new hope. Her father said, "Oh, my boy, you are too young and too smart to give up so soon."

Tom—What made him think you were smart? Had you been showing off?

Bob—No, Tom, I had nothing to "show off" with.

Tom—Well, there is just the difference between you and me. I have got too much "show off" Yes, I go in for "show off;" but you see I have nothing to "show off" with. How did the girl help you—I am anxious to know that?

Bob—She helped me every way, but mostly by *showing me how to save my money.* We were only friends. I made no mention of love to her for more than a year. She was a real sister to me. But I must make my story short. One year ago we were engaged, and in one month we were married. Now, Tom, old boy, you must tell me your story.

Tom sat for some time looking very thoughtful and very much troubled. At length he looked up.

Tom—I have a girl, too, one that I love dearly, and yet she is the one that has cheated me out of an education She wanted to go to parties and entertainments. (We never went to balls, for we are both kind of half way Christians.) She put on a great deal of style and I had to dress to suit Laura, for that is my girl's name. For her sake I learned to show off. It was not naturally in me. Then I had to treat her to every dainty to eat when we were out together. I hired a buggy and went driving. And in so many ways my money was spent. I learned to be fond of fun and frolic, and you know that does not pay.

Bob—I should have been just like you only for Mary. She says she has noticed how thoughtless girls are. They encourage young men to spend money on them that ought to be given to the young men's parents or else go for an education. But, Tom, it is not too late. Have an honest talk with Laura and she will help you, if she loves you.

Tom.—Oh, yes, she loves me and I love her, and we are going to have a "show off" wedding soon. She does not care much for books and yet she is good and kind, and quite intelligent in most ways. But I fear I never will amount to much. My wife's extravagance, like my girl's extravagance will keep me poor. Say, Bob, have you any property? I have none.

Bob—Oh, yes, I have a good house and lot all paid for. Mary will furnish it and we will move right into our little nest the day after we are married. We are to have a quiet wedding. You come and see us. Mary will help you and Laura as she has me. She helps all she meets.

How to get Ready for the Wedding and for Housekeeping.

"Thomas and Mary, I hear that you are to be married next month."

"Yes, that is our plan," they replied hopefully.

"Would you like to have a quiet little talk about the furniture you need for housekeeping, and about that wedding dress and wedding supper, etc.?"

"Yes, that is why we have called," was the answer.

"First, let me know how much money you have on hand, because you must not *go in debt*. I could point you to a dozen young people who bought furniture on time, or in some way went in debt, and lost all, and besides it was not what they *needed*. Sometimes older people buy on trust to make a display, and lose all. This is not only foolish but wicked. You say that both together, you have $100.00. That is right, put your funds *together*. The sooner you learn that marriage is a partnership affair the better it will be for you. It is a foolish idea that the husband must be at *all* the expense of furnishing a home in which the wife has equal rights, and besides require him to buy gold rings and all such foolery. Now we will get a pencil and write down the articles we really need, and what we think the real cost will be, and see if we have enough money for this great transaction." Thomas and Mary smiled and took the pencil and paper I offered them. "Three chairs, one table, and stove and a few plain dishes, enough to set your table decently. Buy a saw and hammer and you can put up a book shelf and other shelves that are necessary, and

out of boxes make seats and cover them with creton.
Out of a box you can fix a washstand and put a cur-
tain around it. Be sure to have a bowl and pitcher,
but buy nothing that is expensive. If you are watchful you can sometimes buy second hand articles that
will serve you as well as the new. It used to be the
opinion of sensible people that a girl was worth but
little who had not prepared quilts, sheets, pillows,
mattress, etc., for a bed before she was 18 years old,
but in those days the girls did not spend as much for
ribbons and jewelry as they do now. These articles
will cost different prices in different localities. Rent,
$5, cooking stove, $12. Table, large enough to serve
for both centre table and dining table, $3. Chairs,
$1.50. Dishes, etc., $5. Saw, axe, hammer and nails,
about $3.50. Total, $30.00. This is supposing that
Mary has her bed all ready; if not, bedstead $4, mat-
tress, $2, other bedding, etc , $5. Of course Mary
has a few articles ready. Total, $41.00. You must
allow $15 for some fuel and provisions. It is a very
extravagant way to buy only a nickel's worth of different kinds of food at one time. When able, lay in
larger quantities when you buy. Preacher's fee and
license will cost at least $5. About the dress. Let
it be very plain and durable so that it can be worn
on any other occasion as well as your wedding day.
Dress, hat, gloves and all, about $15. No money for
long white veil, and white kid gloves. No, not if
you were worth ten times as much money. Do begin
life by dressing in a plain, sensible way, and not according to the fashions of the day, for if you follow
the fashions you will often be in debt, with no *money
for good books, nor time to read,* and nothing left to

help the church and the poor. I know a good girl
that was married in a clean, but not new calico dress,
and she is to-day the best wife and mother, or one of
the best in the world.

Now let us go back to details. Thomas' suit will
cost about $20. We have left, $4. Never spend
every cent you have. In fact you might have gotten
ready for marriage with half the money you have,
and I would do it rather than go in debt, or compel
Mary to go out and cook, or take in washing the day
after you are married, to pay for an extravagant wedding. Of course Mary is to help earn money whenever she can do it and besides keep a house that will
be homelike. I would have no wedding cake nor
supper. If father and mother want to give it to you,
tell them that you would rather have the money to
start life on, and after awhile when money is plenty
we will have a supper. You know that father and
mother are poor, and a supper would be a great tax
on them.

"Only going to be married once in my life," did
you say? Well, that is the *very reason* why you
should marry in a common sense, God-fearing way.
Be very careful to do a thing *right* that can only be
done once.

After marriage as you can save money, get carpet
or matting for your floors. It gives a house a homelike, cozy appearance. Buy other little comforts that
you and Mary will plan for together, which will make
them very dear to you both, but *do not go in debt*.
Mary, I hope you will not be like some wives I know,
always begging your husband for something new—a
dress, hat, or even ask him to bring you candy. He

will find he has nothing but a baby, instead of a wife.

Thomas looked up with such a manly air as if he felt it was his duty to speak for her and exclaimed: " Mary will be sure to do right. I wish I could be as good as she is."

God bless you, Thomas, for those generous words, and may your wife never betray such loving confidence!

With a prayer for God's blessing on their union of hearts and hands we parted. I do not feel at all sure that they will take my advice in all particulars, but they will in some things. I only want to add that if they had $10,000 instead of $100 to begin with, I would counsel strict economy, and never, *never* go in debt one cent. *No, never go in debt.*

Don't Let Mother Do It!

BY CARRIE ALTON.

Daughter, don't let mother do it!
  Do not let her slave and toil,
While you sit a useless idler,
  Fearing your soft hands to soil,
Don't you see the heavy burdens,
  Daily she is wont to bear,
Bring the lines upon her forehead—
  Sprinkle silver in her hair?

Daughter, don't let mother do it!
  Do not let her bake and broil;
Through the long, bright summer hours
  Share with her the heavy toil;
See, her eye has lost its brightness,

Faded from her cheek the glow,
And the step that once was buoyant
Now is feeble, weak, and slow.

Daughter, don't let mother do it!
  She has cared for you so long;
Is it right the weak and feeble,
  Should be toiling for the strong?
Waken from your listless languor,
  Seek her side to cheer and bless;
And your grief will be less bitter,
  When the sods above her press.

Daughter don't let mother do it!
  You will never, never know
What were home without a mother
  Till the mother lieth low—
Low beneath the budding daisies,
  Free from earthly care or pain—
To the home so sad without her,
  Never to return again.

"All Is Not Gold That Glitters."

"Honor to whom is due," reads my Bible. This applies to the respect and attention that young people give to each other while in public, as well as to other relations in life.

FOR THE YOUNG MEN.

To illustrate: Two young ladies, Mary and Jane, are present at a social party. Mary is modest and retiring; she does not know how, and has no desire to put herself forward She is a sensible, good girl, with a pure, unsullied name. Jane is flashy, and dashy, and gay, full of fun and jokes. She will keep all around in laughter, talks nonsense, and knows how to put herself forward on all occasions. She dresses in the fashion at the expense of the hard earnings of her mother, perhaps, or perhaps she earns it herself and spends it *all on herself.* Now every young man present knows that in real worth Mary is far superior to Jane, and yet even the good, sensible young men flock around Jane and leave Mary to sit alone in a neglected corner. This makes our sensible girls often say, " What is the use in being good and modest and sensible? The boys all admire and pay attention to the girls who talk foolishness and fun."

Now, boys, should they not feel a little hurt—feel as if you were not paying honor to whom honor is due? Is it right? Is it any wonder if some of our good, modest girls would try to be silly, and dress gaily so as to *attract your* attention and thereby be led into sin?

Boys, you have a great influence over the girls. If you show a preference for those who selfishly spend time and money for dress and pleasure, and thus neglect home and parents, then you will be the cause of leading many a girl astray. If some day you get one of these silly, selfish women for a wife, I shall not pity you. But suppose you seek out the modest, quiet girl, and pay attention to real worth, then you will make these silly butterflies ashamed of themselves, and many of them will settle down to quiet habits, because they talk their foolishness and dress gaily just to *please you* young men. You ought to be ashamed to discourage virtue and foster vice.

FOR THE YOUNG LADIES.

I remember several young men have written me, "Don't be partial, give the girls their share of reproof and advice." I know the question we are discussing has another side. We will illustrate:

John and James both attend a social gathering. John is a worthy, honest young man, who would rather wear an old coat than go in debt. Besides, he is trying to educate himself and also help his parents. He has no time nor money to spend with fashionable girls. By the way, some who are called sensible girls are very unreasonable with the young men that are their escorts. They expect the gentlemen to treat them to dainties, and take them to expensive places of amusement, even dare to ask a gift for themselves. Oh, girls, I am ashamed of you! In this way you are tempting that young man to spend money on you that he *ought to give to his dear mother.* No good girl will accept a gift from any young man, except a near relative, or one to whom she is engaged, and even then nothing that is very valuable, because after the gift, the young lady does not feel as independent with the young man as she did before. Be womanly, be independent, girls, if you are poor. This is a little off the subject, but it grew out of the fact that John did not spend his money foolishly for the girls, and therefore was not petted and flattered by them. Besides, John does not know how to say foolish, funny, flattering words to the girls. He has no mustache, nor cane, nor does he know how to make an exquisite bow. Of course he is polite and kind, and if the girls had sense enough to sit quietly down and listen, they would find his conversation very interesting and instructive. But over in the other corner of the room is a great attraction. It is our other boy, James. He has the eyes and ears of the girls, as he bows, flatters, and tells foolish stories to make the people laugh. Oh, how they do like to laugh and giggle. How often we give our money freely, just to be amused—a circus or a show will attract the crowd, and James is a kind of circus in himself. You have met such young men, have you not? They dress and have plenty of money, but seldom *honest* money. I have been surprised to see what a power such a silly and even unprincipled young man has over a sensible, good young girl. She will turn off a kind, honest young man, and take the arm of this fashionable fool. I know there is a solid established class of young men and young women who are not attracted by the glitter and dash and folly that I have been describing. They turn away in disgust and seek other company. But there is a large class of young people whose tastes are just being formed. I want to warn them against following such silly, selfish, extravagant leaders in society. Yes, I am sorry to say they are *leaders*, and they are too often flattered and commended in these social gatherings. Sometimes they are real flirts, and have ruined the character or in some way destroyed the happiness of those who believed them true. I call upon all good young men and young women to band themselves together to withdraw the hand of fellowship from all such doubtful characters, and to pay respect and honor to whom honor is due, and thereby elevate the standard of good society and of good morals.

SOCIAL PURITY.

Dear Young Men: I wish to say a few words on the above subject this month. We will first find the meaning of the two words. "Social" means relation and intercourse of a number of human beings who live and work together. Our social life means the life we live with others. When we speak of social happiness we mean the happiness of society in general. Social duties means the duties we owe to each other. Purity in one sense means cleanness or freedom from dirt or filth as might refer to a garment or a house. Again, purity is used to describe freedom from guilt or sin. In the sense I wish to use it, it means chastity—freedom from the things that defile body and soul through the violation of the seventh commandment. The lack of social purity has been a great curse to society for many, many years, but no organization came out to boldly fight it till very lately.

In 1883 good Bishop Lightfoot, of Durham, Eng., organized what was called the White Cross Movement. It soon spread throughout Great Britain, and had branches in Africa, India and Australia. In 1884 the work began in the United States, and it now has an organization in every State in the Union, and in almost every town. Its object is to elevate public opinion in morals, by bringing together in one band all who are pledged to purity and virtue. It is done in a quiet way. Bands of three or five, if not more, can

55

be found, are formed. Tracts are distributed and public lectures are given, sometimes to men and women in separate meetings, sometimes together, according to the character of the lecture.

The first pledge and work was for the men only, but now we have also an organization for the women called the White Shield. In this talk we wish to speak of the work among the men.

White Cross Pledge for Men.

1. I promise to treat all women with respect, and protect them from wrong and degradation.

2. To endeavor to put down all indecent language and coarse jests.

3. To maintain the law of purity as equally binding upon man and woman.

4. To endeavor to spread these principles among my companions, and to try to help my younger brothers.

5. To use every possible means to fulfill the command: " Keep thyself pure."

For many years the press and the pulpit have been too silent on this subject. They scarcely knew how to take hold of it. Ball rooms, card table, saloons, etc., were denounced, and the dens of adultery left untouched. Some, whose ears were more refined than their hearts, said it should not be spoken in public. But they did not learn this false modesty from the Bible. God thundered from Mt. Sinai, " Thou shalt not commit adultery," with the same emphasis that he did " Thou shalt not kill." In Bible narrative, if a man or waman committed adultery, it is recorded, simply because when God writes a man's history he tells the truth, even though it be about the king on his throne. When Paul wrote to the young minister Timothy, he said, "Keep thyself pure," "Flee youthful lusts"; it is not likely that Timothy needed this advice any more than the ministers of to-day do. It would be a good thing if there were more Pauls to-day to teach, to exhort and rebuke the preachers, young and old. Of all men they should be the purest on earth. In virtue of their office, they are admitted into every home, and can sit down by every fireside.

But our lecture to-day is not meant for the ministry, but for *all* young men.

He wants to call attention to one clause in this pledge on social purity.

No. 3. "I promise to maintain the law of purity as *equally* binding upon men and women." In this sin woman has been blamed more than man. There is no authority in God's word for it. It is only a custom or tradition that has bound a heavy burden on poor woman.

Where is that vile coward that won yon young woman's love for the purpose of leading her into sin, and now he has gone and left her alone to care for *his* child. Can you think of anything more dastardly, mean and cowardly than this act? Why did he not stand by her side and share the disgrace? Man is woman's natural protector; but ah, alas! how many times he has betrayed his trust and then left her to suffer alone! Thank God, the young men for whom I write this, do not belong to that vile class. Their character is described in 1st John. 2:14: "I have written unto you young men, because you are strong, and the word of God abideth in you and ye have overcome the wicked one," and because *you are strong* I want you to help the weak ones. "What can we do?" you ask. Copy the pledge for the men on a blank book. I mean this pledge of social purity, and see how many men and boys over twelve years of age you can get to sign it. Urge your young friends to hide God's law in their hearts. Fill their hearts with the Bible. Read Proverbs 6: 20–27. We are told there that God's law will keep us from evil women. Verse 32 of the same chapter says: "He that committeth adultery with a woman, lacketh understanding; he that doeth it destroyeth his own soul." Yes, he does destroy both soul and body. O, young men, do listen to Paul's advice in 2d Timothy, 2:22, and like Paul, "Keep your body under and bring it into subjection," 1st Cor. 9:27. Remember "you can do all things through Christ which strengthens you." Phil. 4:13.

Now, dear young men, do as I have told you. Teach these Bible truths to others, for all do not see the danger that surrounds them. Be faithful, and God will use you to keep many young boys from ever falling into this sin, and help you to save those who have gone astray.

White Shield Pledge for Women.

DEAR YOUNG GIRLS: If you have your dishes washed, and house in order, and your dress neat and clean, then sit down and let us have a quiet talk. You have read the foregoing talk to the young men, and I am sure you were glad that someone said to them what *you could not say*. It seems as if I hardly needed to tell *you* to be modest and ladylike: and yet I have seen *some* girls behave in such a manner that I have to cover my face with shame and even weep bitter tears of sorrow. I want to give you a few words of advice that will keep you from these sinful ways:

First, *Keep the heart pure. An impure thought cherished is a sin.* When a bad thought comes, you should slam the door in its face and not let it in. Phil. 4: 8 gives us a list of subjects to think about. These seven things: Honesty, Truth, Purity, Loveliness, Good Report, Virtue, Praiseworthy. We need not be afraid of others seeing our thoughts on these subjects, need we?

Watch your thoughts when you are alone. If you keep your thoughts pure you will never commit adultery or speak an impure word. The impure thought comes first. Do not think of anything that you would be ashamed to tell your mother or brother or sister.

Now, I know the question you want to ask me, namely, "How can I keep bad thoughts out of my heart?" I am glad I have the answer ready. *Take Jesus into your heart.* His presence will keep all that is bad out.

Second, *Help others to be good.*

I have tried this plan. The greater the effort I make to save others from sin, the more afraid I am to do wrong myself.

I will give you a pledge on purity. Copy it in a blank book, and see how many girls, and women too, you can get to sign it. The girls should be over nine years of age. Explain the pledge to them. Write and ask me, if there be something you do not understand about it.

THE PLEDGE.

I promise with God's help:

1. To reverence all sacred things, and to be modest in language, behavior and dress.

2. To repress all thoughts, words and deeds which I should be ashamed to have my parents know.

3. To avoid all conversation, reading, pictures and amusements which may put wrong thoughts into my mind.

4. To guard the purity and good name of my companions and friends, and never needlessly to speak evil of any, especially when they are absent.

5. To strive after the special blessings promised to the *pure in heart*.

You must do this work quietly and modestly. Read this article to some of the *good* mothers and explain what you want to do and ask their advice. You know there are many *very* good mothers who want their girls to be pure and good: and there are some very careless mothers. Now, we want to help *all* the girls to be good; and when their *own* mothers do not care, then there is all the more need for *you* to help and teach them. Do not be discouraged if you can only get *one* girl to sign the pledge, and if no one will, then work and pray alone.

Has a Man a Better Right to do Wrong than a Woman?

"Is it as wrong for a young man to use bad lan-

guage or lounge around a saloon as it is for a young
lady to do so? Or, in other words, should we require
as high a standard of morals from a young lady as we
do from a young man?" In answer to this question
we say that a man that sins is just as guilty as a
woman, and a woman just as guilty as a man. God
is no respecter of persons.—Acts 10: 34. If any difference is made, we thought that the young man or old
man that has deceived any woman, was often more to
blame than the woman, because man is considered
the strongest and therefore ought to be able to *protect* woman instead of *degrading* her.

Parents, you should begin early to teach your boys
to be manly and pure in thought and word and action.
Teach them to protect their sisters and every woman
from insult. Keep the boys at home as much as possible and shelter them from the company of bad girls.

*Take just as much pains to keep your boys out of
bad company as you do your girls.* If there be a
public meeting of a social or political character
which is not thought to be a proper place for your
daughter, then *keep your son away also.* Impure
words and rough manners will hurt your son just as
much as it will your daughter, and perhaps more.
Modesty and purity are just as much to be desired in
a man as in a woman. Public opinion has been
against the Bible on this subject for many years.
God is no respecter of person. What is a sin for
a woman is also as great a sin for a man. As regards
the sin of adultery the man is the tempter till the
woman has fallen. After that she becomes man's
tempter. Thus, you see, man is *most* to blame,
because by his treachery and unholy love he drags

woman down into the mire of sin. He comes to *that which is pure and good and pollutes it.* When you see a wicked woman standing on the street corners seeking to lure the thoughtless men, young and old, to her " house that takes hold on hell," as described in Prov. 7th, you may be sure that years before some wicked wretch of a man, by his deceit, was the cause of her fall. You can see how important it is, that our boys be taught to control unlawful passions, and keep bad thoughts out of their hearts, or our lessons to the girls will be all in vain.

Now, my dear boy, do not be impatient with mother when she says, " Stay at home with sister and mother. It is not safe to be out so late at night." At least never go away without telling your mother where you are going.

Dear young people, do keep yourselves pure and unspotted from the world. The foundation of a pure life is a pure heart. If Jesus lives and reigns in my soul, his glorious presence will be sure to drive out all that is unholy and impure. " Blessed are the pure in heart for they shall see God." God lives in the pure heart and *only* in the pure heart. Do not let Satan deceive you. Notice if you have low, vulgar thoughts in your heart when you are alone. Do not talk much about things that are impure or bad, but let your conversation be about the good, the beautiful and the pure, and let your own life be right. Then God will make you a great blessing in purifying society.

TEMPERANCE.

"The First Glass."

Every man, woman and child ought to know the danger of taking the "first glass" of intoxicating liquor. Those who never take the first glass *cannot* take the second, and therefore they are safe. I wish I could get this down deep into the hearts of all mothers. Then they would never give their babies one drop of toddy, nor take it themselves. Liquor would be banished entirely from all homes.

WHERE DID THE DRUNKARD BEGIN.

Answer—with

> Glass number one,
> Only in fun;
> Glass number two,
> Other boys do;
> Glass number three,
> It won't hurt me;
> Glass number four,
> Only one more;
> Glass number ten,
> Drinking again;
> Glass number twenty,
> Not yet a plenty;
> Drinking with boys,
> Drowning his joys;
> Drinking with men,
> Just now and then;

Wasting his life,
Killing his wife;
Losing respect,
Manhood all wrecked;
Losing all friends—
Thus it all ends.
Glass number ONE ruined his life.

WARNING TO THE YOUNG.

Light-hearted boy, somebody's joy,
Do not begin thus to sin;
But grow up a man, brave as you can,
Taste not in fun ' Glass number ONE.'

—Selected.

Robbery.

Some persons argue that it is unjust to hinder any one from buying and drinking intoxicating liquors. "If they want it let them have it," say they. Here is the argument in poetry. Read it and see if it makes you a Prohibitionist or not.

What! rob a poor man of his beer,
    And give him good victuals instead—
Your heart's very hard, sir, I fear,
    Do you think we can live upon bread?

What! rob a poor man of his mug,
    And give him a house of his own,
With kitchen and parlor so snug?
    'Tis enough to draw tears from a stone.

What! rob a poor man of his glass,
    And teach him to read and to write!

What! save him from being an ass?
  'Tis nothing but teetotal spite!

What! rob a poor man of his ale,
  And prevent him from beating his wife,
From being locked np in jail,
  Or in a penitentiary for life!

           —*Spurgeon.*

Temperance Pledge.

We would advise every young person to sign a pledge. It is a safeguard against taking the *first* glass, which is really the first step in drunkenness. One glass puts you *under the influence of liquor* as far as one glass has the power, and therefore you are *one glass drunk.* When asked in public or private to take a little wine, beer, etc., just say,"no I cannot; I am pledged to temperance." Any one who is really a gentleman or lady will nct ask you to break your pledge. I have known so many young people who have been saved in the midst of great temptation because of a solemn promise they made when very young. I remember something that occurred in New Orleans about twenty-one years ago. Four young men were in my Sabbath school; two would not sign the temperance pledge because they said, "There is no danger, I know how to govern myself, I will make no promise." Two signed. Twelve years after, I met one of my temperance young men who then had a lovely wife and four children and *owned* a good home in New Orleans. Said he, " That temperance pledge saved me and my friend. Both those other young men who would not sign have been ruined by

strong drink and bad company. The temperance
pledge kept us out of the saloon and away from bad
company." The history of these young men is only
one example out of a hundred that I could give. It
is true some sign and break their pledge, but that
does not prove the pledge wrong, any more than it
proves that uniting with a church or marriage is
wrong, because some backslide, and others are not
true to their marriage vows. I wish every young
person male and female would *take and keep* the following

PLEDGE.

I promise, by the help of God, to abstain from the
use of all intoxicating liquors, and to do all in my
power to keep others from using the same; also, to
abstain from tobacco in every form, and from all pro-
fanity, gambling and Sabbath breaking.

Sister's Advice.

Don't drink it, Tom, don't drink it,
Put the tempting glass aside;
Remember what you promised, Tom,
When our dear mother died.
Remember her sweet counsel,
When our earnest life began;
Come out in God's bright sunshine, Tom,
Come out, and be a man.

Don't drink it, Tom, don't drink it,
If you do, you'll thirst for more;
'Twill rob you of your senses, Tom,
As once it did before.
Your blood is young and ardent,

As your heart is pure and true;
Oh! listen to my pleading, Tom,
Strong drink is not for you.

Don't drink it, Tom, don't drink it,
Put the tempting glass aside;
Refuse it for her sake, dear Tom,
Who soon will be your bride.
Oh! make the future happy,
Of your darling if you can.
Come out in God's bright sunshine, Tom,
Come out and be a man.

—Selected.

If I Would Not Be a Drunkard.

———

(Tune " I Want to be An Angel.")

If I would not be a drunkard
  I must not drink a drop
Of the wine that looks so tempting,
  Within the ruby cup.
For such a small beginning,
  Though innocent it seem,
May lead me on to sinning
  More fearful than I dream.

If I would not be a drunkard,
  I stoutly must refuse
All the sorts of beer and cider
  Which other people use.
They may not steal my reason,
  But they will give the taste,
And lead me on when older,
  To hanker for the rest.

If I would not be a drunkard,
  I must not smoke or chew,

For they say these evils habits
    Will lead to drinking too.
And I must shun companions
    With words and actions vile,
Or else my feet will surely
    Slide downward all the while.

If I would not be a drunkard,
    I must the Lord obey,
I must flee from all tempation,
    And ever watch and pray.
His loving arms can keep me,
    From evil and from sin,
And lead me on to heaven,
    The crown of life to win.

[Selected.]

GOOD MANNERS.

Always knock before entering the door of a private house or private room. Never knock at the door of a store, hotel, church, or any public place of business; where people are expected, it is not necessary to give warning before entering.

Always remove the hat when you enter a private house, or public parlor, or church. Lift your hat when speaking to a lady. You do this as a matter of respect to the people of the place or to the place.

In handing a tool or vessel to any one, always present it so that they can take hold of the handle.

Doctors tell us that the chewing of gum or any substance is very injurious to the health; but aside from this, it is very impolite to be seen chewing gum or eating anything in company unless it can be shared with the company. For this reason do not eat candy, nuts, etc., in public places.

Never read the letters of other people unless invited to do so.

Never look over the shoulder of any one who is reading or writing.

Never lend a book, or anything that is borrowed, unless special permission has been given you.

Interrupting the speech of others is a great sin against good maners. Be more ready to listen than to speak.

Never assume a lounging position in company, but sit erect. Do not twist your arms and feet around your chair; nor stretch out your arms and yawn or gap, if you can help it.

If you want to appear awkward, be always thinking about yourself and how you look. When in company forget yourself and your dress, and try to be interested in what others are saying and doing,

"Politeness is to do and say
The kindest thing in the kindest way."

And everything that is unkind is un=Christian. To seek the happiness and welfare of others is true politeness.

When I was young I learned to say these two lines at night:

"Did I this day for great or small my own pursuits
    forego,
Or lighten by a feather's weight the mass of human
    woe?"

The following verses teach the same sweet thought:

"If we sit down at set of sun
And count the things that we have done,
    And counting find
One self=denying act, one word
That eased the heart of him who heard,
    One glance most kind
That fell like sunshine where it went.
Then we may count that day well spent."

Bible rule: "Whatsoever ye would that men should do unto you, do ye even so unto them." Matt 7: 12.

RULES FOR DAILY LIFE.

Begin the day with God;
    Kneel down to him in prayer;
Lift up thy heart to his abode,
    And seek his love and care.

Open the Book of God,
  And read a portion there;
That it may hallow all thy thoughts
  And sweeten all thy care.

Go through the day with God,
  Whate'er thy work may be;
Where'er thou art at home, abroad,
  He is still near to thee.

Converse in mind with God;
  Thy spirit heavenward raise;
Acknowledge every good bestowed,
  And offer grateful praise.

Then end the day with God;
  Thy sins to him confess;
Trust in the Lord's atoning blood,
  And plead his righteousness.—*Selected*

Table Manners.

1. Sit erect and close to the table.

2. Notice if others are passing their plates and wait till they are served.

3. Ask quietly and politely for what you want.

4. Never eat till you cannot eat any more. Only a glutton does that.

5. Do not allow yourself to be helped to more than you can eat. This is economy.

6. Eat slowly and gently. Pass your food to your mouth with a fork or spoon.

7. Never ask to be served twice to dessert or any delicacy unless you are sure there is a great plenty.

8. Do not cut, but break your bread, and only take a small piece in your hand or on your plate at once.

Always lift and pass food to others courteously, and never shove it across the table. Avoid putting your own knife, spoon or fork into any dish but your own.

9. Make as little noise in eating as possible. Keep the lips closed while eating.

10. Chew your food well.

11. Don't talk with your mouth full.

12. Drink as little as possible with your meals.

13. Be cheerful. Notice the pleasant things, the things that are right.

14. If an accident happens, take as little notice of it as possible. "Accidents will happen in the best regulated families."

15. Should a certain article of food disagree with you, do not feel that it is necessary to mention this fact, or enter into any explanations. Decline with thanks.

16. If it is necessary to remove any obstruction from between the teeth let it be done in a quiet manner, holding the napkin before the mouth with the left hand. Even this is to be avoided if possible.

17. Do not rest your arms nor your hands on the table. In cutting your food be careful to keep your arms close to your side.

18. When through eating put your knife and fork together on the right side of your plate.

What is Politeness?

I will give you a splendid rule of politeness taken from the Bible, "Be kindly affectioned one to another with brotherly love, in honor preferring one another."

Rom. 12: 10. There is a rough, saucy, rude way of showing affection which is not polite, is not kind. If you give your seat to another or step back so as to give them the best place, or help them in any way, do it *quietly* so as to not call the attention of others to what you have done. Please notice when you enter a room and do not take the easy chair or best seat. I was much grieved the other day by seeing a young girl seat herself in the arm chair when there were four ladies in the room older than she was. I have also seen a young man behave in the same thoughtless way. A polite person is always anxious to give others the best. Our verse says " in honor preferring one another," that means that we prefer or decide to give others the most honorable position. I wish you would notice how impolite some young persons are in the street cars and on the sidewalks; they will hardly step aside to let you pass. Have you ever seen a young man or woman in company who seemed very anxious to do all the talking themselves? This is very rude, very impolite. Give others a chance. Suppose you and another of the company know the same story, request your friend to tell it rather than hear yourself talk. I want to repeat it, polite persons are the ones who try to make others happy and comfortable. They avoid doing anything that they know will annoy or grieve any one, and yet if asked to do what is wicked they firmly but quietly and politely refuse. To illustrate: John wants James to take a pleasure ride on Sunday. James is a Christian and he replies, "It is very kind in you to invite me and I thank you for it, but I believe the Sabbath is a day in which to worship God and study his word, it is not a day to seek my own pleasure. You will forgive me for not going out with you; I should like to be with you, but can't you come with me to the young people's meeting?" This polite refusal has won John, and he takes James' arm and walks with him to the house of God. Take another illustration: Henry says to Thomas, "Come let us go in here and get a glass of beer." Thomas flares up and says, "Henry, you are on the road to hell, you will a drunkard before long; I am ashamed to walk the streets with you." Henry is displeased, he will not listen to God's message from the friend that answered him thus rudely. The religion of the Lord Jesus makes us gentle and patient and loving, and this is true politeness. Another Bible rule is "Let every one of us please his neighbor for his good to edification." Rom. 15: 2. Notice it must be for *his good* and to edify or build up. Never do wrong to please any one, but if you must differ, do it in a polite way. I wish you would also notice Rom. 15: 1. "We then that are strong ought to bear the infirmities of the weak, and not to please ourselves." This will make you very gentle and polite to the little children, to the poor, to the ignorant and to all who are weaker than you are. Dear young people, please remember the advice I have given you in this article, it comes from a heart that loves you dearly.

Be on Time and keep Your Promise.

No one will succeed in any business who is in the habit of being late. It seems to me that I have lost at least three years of the last twenty-five years of my life in waiting on persons who promised to meet me at a certain hour and did not come until long after the time. Perhaps it was a meeting, then, not only myself but many others lost time. If fifty waited one half an hour then fifty times one half an hour was lost. You say, "Begin and do not wait on the tardy ones." But if I do, these slow folks will come in and interrupt the best part of the meeting. It might be a good plan to lock the door and send those home who come late. Those who are not *on time* are both thieves and liars. They promised to come and did not keep their word. Is not that a falsehood? They have stolen my time. Time is worth more than any earthly possession, therefore, those who steal time are the *worst* thieves.

Do learn promptness while young. Let me tell you what often steals time and causes you to be late: 1st. Idleness, downright laziness, steals time. 2nd. Foolish gossip, listening to idle tales, steals time. 3rd. Disorder, careless habits, that lead you to *waste* time in hunting for articles when needed, which is just the same as stealing your time. 4th. Trying to follow the foolish fashions of the world, as regards dress and amusements, steals your time and leads you into sin. If you will strive to avoid the above wicked habits and use your time wisely then you can always be *on time* for all that is good and right. It is said George Washington and Benjamin Franklin never kept any one waiting, but were always up to the very minute in keeping an engagement. And so it will be with all good and great people who have learned the value of time; they will not steal it from others, nor waste it themselves. One word more on this subject of promising and not keeping your promise. It is sinful; it is a great injury both to yourself and the one to whom you have made the promise. A teacher who had tried to establish a school in a certain town told me these words: "Since I have been here, I think about seventy-five persons have promised to come to my school, who did not come, nor have any of these people come to me to make an apolgy for not keeping their word. This has been a great hindrance to me and kept me here, when I might have gone elsewhere and gotten a school." I can say with this gentleman that I have often been hindered by this same kind of promises, that mean nothing, and are really a *falsehood*. Surely such persons have forgotten that the Bible says, " All liars shall have their part in the lake which burneth with fire and brimstone." If you can't do what you are asked to do, then say *no*, promptly, and decidedly, and if you are disappointed and really could not do what you *intended* to do, then send or bring an apology as soon as possible.

Nothing.

I asked a lad what he was doing;
  "Nothing, good sir, " said he to me.
"By nothing well and long pursuing,
  Nothing," said I, "you'll surely be."

I asked a lad what he was thinking;
  "Nothing," quoth he, "I do declare."
"Many," said I, "in taverns drinking,
  By idle minds are carried there."

There's nothing great, there's nothing wise,
  Which idle hands and minds supply;
Those who all thought and toil despise,
  Mere nothings live, and nothings die.

—Selected.

How to do Business.

Keep an exact account of all you *earn* and all you *spend.* Then settle up or square accounts at the close of each month or better at the end of each week. This will enable you to to see clearly *two important facts:* First, for *what you have spent your money;* Second, *Are you in debt?* Do not say that keeping such an account will take too much time. I can assure you that you will save time and money by this plan. Only a very few persons can tell *exactly* for what they have spent every cent of what they have earned, hence they do not stop to think and plan for what is the *most important articles to purchase.* We want girls as well as boys, and women as well as men to keep these accounts. Those who cannot write but have children who can, should train them to keep the accounts for their parents. Little children, as soon as they are able to write should be entrusted with a little money and taught how to use it. Money is talent. Money is power. We must one day give an account to God for the way in which it was used. Let me illustrate the value of keeping an itemized record of how money is spent. A little girl eight years old who had learned how to write was trusted with ten cents each week to spend as she thought best. Her wise parents, hoping in

this way to train her to the *right* use of money.
Each week child and parent examined the account
book together at the end of a month it was found
that our little Susie had spent ten cents for a nice
book and the other thirty cents for candy and nuts.
The parents made no criticism but simply said:
"Susie do you think you have made good use of
your money? Susie stopped to think a few minutes
and then said: "My candy and nuts were soon eaten
up, but I have my nice book and have had it every
day. Next month I will spend for things I *can
keep*." You see this was *one* important lesson
learned by Susie, because she saw *where* her money
went. Of course as the days passed by wise parents
would suggest ways of helping others with her
money.

Such an exact record of receipts and expenses will
show if you are in debt. No one but a wicked
spendthrift will plunge himself in debt, but he will
carefully look over his accounts and see what it is
possible to do without and deny himself rather than
go in debt.

I asked a girl who was out at service and earned
$10 per month: "How do you spend your money?"
"I do not know but it all goes somewhere" was her
reply. I showed her how to keep accounts and *urged*
her to put down every cent she spent. As a result at
the end of six months she had money enough saved to
attend school three months. You should always take
a receipt when you pay a debt be it ever so small an
amount. I knew a man who lost two hundred dollars
in the purchase of his home because he lost one of
his receipts and neglected to get a receipt twice.

Young people are especially thoughtless about money. They forget "a penny saved is as good as a penny earned." Your time and money is worth more now than it will be when you are older. The beauty of summer, the fruitfulness of autumn and the support of winter, all depends upon the seed sowed in the springtime. Notice carefully how you spend your nights and your Sabbath days. There is where the waste usually begins, of money, time and strength. Now, remember, keep accounts, take receipts and be careful not to lose your business papers. NEVER GO IN DEBT.

ECONOMY.

"Spare Moments."

Dear Young Friends: I wish I knew what you do in your leisure moments, or in other words, your play-time. I mean when you are let loose from your regular business or daily labor. What do you do? say on Sabbath or during Christmas holidays? What do you do with the time, that is *your own* to use as you please? Every one, however busy, has a few minutes that they call their own, Now, how do you spend those few minutes? That is what I want to know. If I knew that, I could read your character, I could tell what kind of a man or woman or boy or girl you are.

My dear young friends, it is these spare moments that will *make* or *break* you. Some boys as soon as daily tasks are over, loaf around the street corners or hunt up an idle companion with whom they can laugh and talk foolishness. Other boys seek companion-ship of good and wise people, of whom they can learn as well as enjoy innocent fun, or they take a good book and study, or else they will put up a shelf for mother or mend a broken chair, or in some way help or comfort their neighbor, or some member of their family.

I know a girl who spends all her spare minutes in putting trimming either on her hat or dress and in seeing which looks the prettiest, or she goes off to visit and walk the streets. I do not mean that it is wrong to visit. Oh, no, I believe in being sociable. But it is the *kind* of company you choose that does the harm or good. I have known a husband that would come home, eat supper and then take his hat and go to his neighbor's house and gossip till ten o'clock at night, and leave his own wife and children to mourn his thoughtlessness, or perhaps I ought to say unkindness. When this husband was a boy at home, I am quite sure he did not like to spend his evenings at home with his mother and sisters. Girls, I would be afraid to marry a man that was not kind and obliging to his mother and sisters and little brothers. Boys, I want you to beware of the girl who lets her mother do all the drudgery of the house work, and when she has a spare moment she spends it all for her own gratification and never thinks of the comfort of others, or one that is always teasing her mother for something new to wear, or else she wants to attend some place of amusement. I fear such a girl would not make a good wife.

I know a young man who works hard, and all his *spare* money as well as *spare* time he gives to his mother and sisters. He often gives them presents of little articles that make their work easier, or their home more comfortable. One Christmas he gave his mother an easy chair. If I were a girl I would "set my cap" for that young man. I think you see how your manner of spending your spare moments indicates your true character. They show what you enjoy, what you have a natural taste for. Your daily employment may not be what you choose, but only what you must do in order to make a living, but what

you do in your spare moments *is what you choose,*
and for that reason it is a test of your real worth.
Young people, I wish you would watch yourselves in
this matter and tell me if I am correct. Notice also
your thoughts when *alone,* for that is another test of
your character.

Be Saving.

Dear Young People:—I want to talk to you about
economy—saving your money, in order to buy a
home and have it comfortably furnished, or save, so
that you can get an education, or to buy good books
and have time to read them. These words are mostly
for the boys, and yet the girls do so much to make
the boys extravagant. Girls should not let the young
men spend so much money on them. I mean in taking them to places of amusement and such like. I
hope none of the girls who read this book *accept* gifts
from young men, or worse still, *ask* for them. But I
have known girls who did so. But it is not right. If
you are engaged to the young man urge him to save
his money so that when you are married you can
have a comfortable home.

I had thought to tell the young girls not to marry a
young man who had no prospect of being able to support her so that she could stay at home and make
that home cozy and homelike for her husband; but I
fear the girls would not obey me. They marry often
when they know they will be required to support the
man they marry. I want to tell you what has led me
to think along this line. I find so many wives and
mothers who must work out and get the bread for her

husband and children, and yet that husband is not always a drunkard nor is he lazy, but he does not know how to save to a good advantage what he earns, and his wife is like him in this respect. It takes far more brains and heart to *spend* money properly than it does to *earn* it. We are too fond of eating rich food; too fond of things that taste good.

It is surprising to see how many will come out to a supper and pay well for it, and yet the same persons will not, cannot pay twenty-five cents for a good book. I do want you to be saving of your money. The old saying, "A penny saved is as good as a penny earned," is true, and yet it is not believed. I found the following narrative about "'Tis but" boxes, that I want you to read and get such a box. Be saving with your nickels and you will soon have dollars. I am so sorry for the women and children that have no comfortable homes to-day. This is why I am warning the young people.

"'TIS BUT" BOXES.

The doctrine of thrift, of avoiding useless expenditure and putting aside something for the future, cannot be too often taught. We do not see how important it is to save the "littles." A celebrated New York financier lately related this incident out of his own experience.

"Some years ago I took a great fancy to a young man. He was getting a good salary, but though he was not wickedly extravagant, he could never save a cent.

"Finally he married, and I thought that perhaps the responsibilities of wedded and family life would induce him to pay more attention to the limitations of his purse. Such was not the case, however, and what made the matter worse, his wife seemed to be quite as heedless as her husband in this respect. They were fast drifting upon the rocks of bankruptcy.

"Then he came to me with the story of his troubles. I told him that when I was a boy it was the custom in Peekskill to have a ' 'Tis But' box—a box in which should be deposited all the quarters and other pieces which otherwise would be spent for this or that on the plea, ' Well, 'tis but a nickel, 'tis but a dime, 'tis but a quarter;' or, ' 'Tis but a half dollar.'

"The young man went home and made such a box forthwith; his wife took kindly to the notion, and in a year he brought me a thousand dollars which he desired me to invest for him.

"A general distribution of ' 'Tis But' boxes would be a blessing to the community."—*Youth's Companion.*

Debt.

"Owe no man anything but to love one another."—Rom. 13: 8.

I am glad that the only debt I am required to have is a debt of love. It is a beautiful thought. God's love for me has been so great in the past, and is constantly being poured into every part of my being—so full, so free—and the only way I can pay it back is by loving others. This I cannot do as fully as God loves me. Therefore the debt is never paid in that sense. Then as God is constantly giving me his love and tenderness and patience, I am in debt too constantly to give it out, no matter how it is received by others. What a sweet mission we have here on earth! Pouring out from morn to night the love that God pours into us. Praise his name! May the Lord deliver us from all other kinds of debt.

Money debt is not only dishonest but it is cruel and unkind. There is no other sin so far reaching in its curse as that of debt. B cannot pay C because A *will not* pay B, therefore C cannot pay D, and so on to the end of the alphabet. It upsets all order in society, and brings confusion everywhere.

I met poor neighbor John this evening. His employer would not or could not pay him his wages at the end of the mouth as he promised, therefore there was nothing left for John to do but go in debt to his washerwoman, his grocer, his milkman, his butcher, the dry goods man, everywhere he is in debt now. Just because that *one* man owes John, John is obliged to owe everyone upon whom he depends. These persons of whom John buys on trust must go in debt also, because John did not pay them. What a shame, what a sin for the man who *began* this trouble by not paying the wages when earned!

But the question is asked: Was it John's duty to go in debt to all these persons because one man did not pay him? I answer *no*, it was not right for John to go in debt. Two wrongs will never make one right· He should have gone home and said, "wife, we must live on what we have in the house. I will not go in debt for food any more than I would steal it. The Bible forbids both, and I will obey the Lord if I starve." The next day he can tell his employer, " My Bible will not allow me to go in debt. You did

not pay me my wages, therefore my children are cry-
ing for bread at home to-day." If all the laborers
would do this, then the man that owns the establish-
ment would either get the money or sell out to one
who would pay promptly. But we all go right along
in this wicked way till we become so hardened as not
to *feel we have sinned* when we do not pay our debts.
I know so many persons who care so little about debt
that when they do have money they spend it foolishly
for what they *do not need* rather than try to pay their
honest debts. This is downright dishonest, and God
has them down on his book as thieves.

Let us be saving of our money. Never buy what
we do not *need* or we will soon *need what we cannot
buy.*

The John mentioned in this paper represents a
great multitude who suffer extreme want, and all
because the money they have earned is not paid
promptly. Read Deut. 24:1–15, and you will see that
wages should be paid at the end of each day, if required. This matter of debt includes paying for what
I purchase the same as paying laborers If I buy an
article and do not pay for it, then I am a thief. I
hope all our readers will give this subject of debt
much prayerful consideration and decide and obey
the just and honest way. I praise the Lord for making me see the sin of debt when I was very young,
therefore I have never been one cent in debt in all
my life. Dear young people, you are just beginning
life; beware of debt, it has ruined many.

FASHION.

Dress.

There are two subjects that always interest young women and people in general, namely, Dress and Marriage. They are as old as the garden of Eden, and will never lose their interest till we arrive in the Heavenly Paradise where all are clothed in the one same spotless Robe of Christ's Righteousness, and "where there is neither marrying nor giving in marriage, but all are the sons of God." But down in this lower world these are subjects of very great importance.

We will let the men dress as they please for the present, but girls, I want you to come and sit down beside me, and let us have a little plain talk on this subject of dress.

The dress of a lady decides her character in the eyes of others to a very great extent. *Not the quality*, but the way it is made, and the way she wears it. It may be silk or calico, it matters but little what it is. If a lady has a lot of ribbons and laces strung around her, and piles of flowers on her hat, her dress weighed down with flounces, and drapery that makes you tired to think of her carrying it all day long, then you know this woman cares a great deal for show, and is very anxious to have others admire her. If there is a hole or slit in her dress, buttons torn off, shoes unlaced, etc., then we know she is slovenly and will not make a good housekeeper, she will not keep things in order. If her dress is soiled—covered with grease spots, and hair uncombed—then we know this is a dirty woman, and we would not like to live with her, nor eat her cooking. A young man would know if he had her for his wife that he would never nave a nice clean shirt to wear, nor his clothes brushed. He would be known in the gates as the man that had a dirty wife. Prov. 31–23.

But suppose, young girls, that you have only a calico dress made neatly, sewing well done, not much trimming, gloves with no holes, buttons all on the shoes, hat not showy but plain, the shape that becomes you. If there is not a grease spot or soiled place to be found on any part of your dress, then all who see you will say: There is a lady, a good housekeeper, clean, neat, orderly; she has a place for everything, and everything in its place. She will not waste time in hunting things. Her dress does not cost much. She will not be extravagant. She is not vain nor fond of show. That is what the *careful* observer will read from your dress.

Your dress tells if you are a saving or an extravagant woman, if you are cleanly or a dirty woman, if you are a modest person or immodest, if you have good or bad taste, if you are orderly or disorderly. It tells if you are fond of praise and flattery, or if you are quiet and want to keep out of sight. It tells if you are proud and haughty, or if you are humble.

You did not think, dear young ladies, that your dress had so many tongues and could say so much, or you would have taken more pains to dress right. Your dress talks as you walk along the street, as you sit in church and while you do your work at home, as you sit talking to a friend, your dress talks too You can't stop its talking.

This question of dress is a question of morals, a question of right or wrong. If a young girl even has the money, she should not dress extravagantly for show, for it creates envy and that is sinful. Her neighbor that sees her rigged up will want the same dress and make her mother unhappy by teasing for a dress or hat like May or Jane wears. In this way you lead the other girls into temptation. If she cannot get the clothes she wants then she may run away from home so as to work and earn fine dresses.

Love of dress has ruined many a girl. Love of dress, not only by girls, but also by their mother's, is one great reason why our daughters are not educated. Mothers will say, I must have my girl dress like the other girls, or she is not going out even to Sunday school. I can't make her see that this is conforming to the world and disobeying God. Rom. 12-1, 2. But it is a real sin.

If I had the money wasted in dress, not really needed, money that they might have saved from dress, I could have educated many a girl now in ignorance.

Dear girls, why do you want to be rigged out like that empty headed girl strutting along the streets like a peacock showing off its feathers? Your youth, your young bright face is a sweet ornament in itself, and all the rich clothes and trimming you hang on you lessens that beauty. The plainer and less expensive our dress, provided it be neat and clean, the better our influence over others. We make the poor satisfied with their plain dress, and we ourselves, if we are rich, can save our money to do good. Besides the Bible forbids the wearing of gold and costly apparel. 1st Tim. 2-9.

Our dress must be modest, not showy. The real beauty is inside. "The hidden man of the heart. Meek and quiet spirit." 1st Pet. 3-3, 4. But this beauty is hidden by showy, costly clothes. It can't shine out through a lot of jewelry, ribbons, and flounces.

Oh, girls, dear girls, do listen to what I have said about dress, and save your money and educate that "inner man," the heart and soul. The king's daughters are all glorious within. Bad thoughts and bad actions will make your face ugly. "The ornament of a meek and quiet spirit" makes you pretty in the sight of God, and also in the sight of all good people.

Let your outward dress be plain and cost but little, and save your money and get an education that will make you more and more lovely as the years go by. This dress will not fade.

Heavenly Feet and Heavenly Waists for Women.

In China the women have a very foolish idea of beauty as respects the foot. They think a small foot is very lovely. We are a little like them, because sometimes we pinch our toes with tight shoes. When quite young a Chinese mother puts a bandage around the little girl's foot and binds it tight, so that the foot can grow no larger. This is very painful, but the child must submit in order to have a beautiful(?) foot, but the result of this foolish practice is that Chinese women can hardly walk at all, because they have such little stubs of feet that are not able to bear the weight of the body. There are some Chinese men who do not like women with small feet. They wanted wives whose feet were just the size that nature intended they should be; therefore these young men formed a society called the "heavenly feet society." All who joined it promised to marry only such women as would let their feet grow as large as heaven wanted them to grow. I do not know how much good this society has done.

A good and intelligent woman has suggested to the young men of America that they form a "heavenly waist" society, and promise that they will not marry a woman who does not let her waist grow as large as God wants it to grow. She hopes thereby to stop the girls from their foolish practice of lacing or wearing dresses so tight that the vital organs of their being cannot do their work, and therefore they soon grow into sick and helpless women. Small waists destroy the health and deform the body much more than do small feet. Girls what will you do about it? How many of you will promise to make your dresses loose, and let your waists grow as large as nature intended them to grow? But I had better say, mothers what will you do about it? You are the persons who can remedy this evil quicker than can the girls; you have the controlling and training of your girls, and you know how quickly tight dresses will destroy the health of your daughters.

Fashion.

Dear Young People:—You are now in the spring time of life. You that are farmers know what we do in the spring. It is the time for preparing the ground and sowing the seed; and we always want the very best seed we can get, because the harvest depends largely upon the character of the seed sown. It is impossible to get a good harvest from bad seed. Therefore never say, "I am sowing my wild oats." If you sow wild oats you will reap wild oats in old age, unless God gives you a chance to pull them up and plant the ground over again, and even then it may be too late to raise a crop. Oh, dear young people, do not idle or misspend the morning of life. Be careful to sow good seed in your young hearts.

When our mothers were together in council, they planned that they would not try to follow the fashions in dressing their children, but would dress them according to comfort and health. Now I would like to know what the young people think on the subject. But first we must understand what is meant by fashion. Fashion means the ways or customs of worldly people. If we accept this definition, then Christian young people should not follow the world.

Rom. 12: 2 says, "Be not conformed to this world, but be ye transformed by the renewing of your mind, that ye may prove what is that good and acceptable and perfect will of God." To conform means to form your dress or your talk, or the food you eat, or whatever you do, to the world. Yes, do as the people around you do. This is conforming to the world. There is an old saying that contradicts this text I have given you, which says, "When you are in Rome you must do as the Romans do," and I hear this quoted as a rule of action much oftener than I hear the bible rule, Rom. 12: 2. I am told you must dress as others do, so that you will not look "peculiar," so they may not notice how you are dressed. But this advice contradicts a verse in my Bible, 1st Pet. 2:9, where we are called a "peculiar poeple." Yes, I must dress in a way to show forth the praises of God and not the praises of a fashionable dressmaker, or the wicked people who make the fashions, and who make them different every year so that I must take my money to make a new dress or make my old one over, and thereby I spend my money to please the world and not to please God. Read 1st Pet. 2: 9, and also hunt out all its references in a reference Bible. We must *not* try to look like the world nor act like the world, because we want to get the people away from worldliness and bring them to Christ. "Ye cannot serve God and mammon." Get the most durable material that you can afford for your dress, and make it in a way that gives you comfort, and with as little show as possible; keep it always clean and neat, but do not try to get it made in the latest style unless you want to please the world, and waste your money, and displease God.

I said to the people at the sister's meeting in Searcy, Ark., in 1893, that love for fashionable dress had deprived hundreds of young girls of the benefit of a good education, and none there could deny it. These girls would use their money for gay, fashionable dress instead of for books and board while at school. To get their dress took thought, time, and money, therefore these girls are ignorant women to-day. I have watched this performance for more than forty years, and I am prepared to say that fashion is a great hindrance to the spiritual and intellectual elevation of any race, and I do beg and beseech our young people to give less attention to fashionable dress, but have all your garments whole and clean, and pay more attention to your soul and to your brains and you will be a blessing to your race, and to all the world.

Fashion does not only refer to dress. If we talk and act like the world we are following the fashions of the world. Suppose we go to balls or parties where worldly people enjoy themselves, then we are in the fashion. When in company we are afraid to introduce the subject of religion because it is not the fashion. Like some of the pupils of my school and of our different Bible bands, they are ashamed to carry even a Bible with them, because it is not the fashion of the world to do so, and they are almost ashamed to be seen reading it because it is not the fashion. I wish we had the courage of a little boy named Harry, who went to spend a few weeks with his uncle. The next day after he arrived he heard his uncle and his boys swear or say some bad words. Harry went up to his uncle and with great earnestness said: "Uncle, I must go home, I can't stay here." "What is wrong, Harry? I thought you were going to stay three weeks," asked his uncle. "Mother does not allow me to keep company with anyone who says bad words, and you and the boys say bad words, and so I must leave and go home." The poor uncle was conscience stricken, and putting his arms around this brave little Christian, said: "Harry, my dear boy, stay with us and help us to be good and we will quit saying bad words."

May God give all our boys and girls Harry's courage to reprove sin instead of conforming to it. This is what is meant by standing up for Jesus. It does not mean simply speaking in meeting. It means living a pure, holy life in the " midst of a wicked and perverse nation, among whom ye shine as lights in the world, holding forth the word of life." Phil. 2: 15–16.

A Beautiful Woman.

In a little white house on a hillside green,
Lives as beautiful woman as ever was seen,
In the sixty-five years that she has lived I may say,
She's been growing more beautiful every day.
You do not believe it? ask Susie my sister.
This lovely woman's the first one that kissed her,
And if she'd not nursed her by night and day,
Poor Sue would have been in a very bad way.
I can bring other witnesses whom you may face,
They will tell you the same—they were in the same
        place;
Has she lovers? Yes surely no less than eleven.
She has seven on earth and four more up in heaven.
Her hair is so beautiful —faded and thin;
There are beautiful wrinkles from forehead to chin.
Her eyes are charming as charming can be,
When she looks o'er her glasses so fondly at me.
And I know by her life which has beautiful been,
She is like the King's daughter—"all glorious within."
Ah! you have guessed who it is, it could be no other
Than my beautiful, darling old mother."

I do not know who wrote the above verses, but I dearly love them, and I have given them to the young people, thinking it might make us all more careful of our "darling old mothers." Let us love them with a love true and strong, and tenderly nurse and pet them as they nursed and petted us when we were young. Be patient with both father and mother when they are old.

OBEDIENCE.

Write Your Parents a Letter.

Don't go to the party, the lecture or ball,
    But stay in your room to-night;
Deny yourself to the friends that call,
    And a good long letter write—
Write to the sad old folks at home,
    Who sit when the day is done,
With folded hands and downcast eyes,
    And think of the absent one—
      Write them a letter to-night.

Don't selfishly scribble, " Excuse my haste;
    I've scarcely time to write,"
Lest their brooding thought go wandering back
    To many a bygone night
When they lost their needed sleep and rest,
    And every breath was a prayer
That God would leave their delicate babe
    To their tender love and care—
      Write them a letter to-night.

Don't let them feel that you've no more need
    Of their love and council wise;
For the heart grows strangely sensitive
    When age has dimmed the eyes.
It might be well to let them believe
    You never forgot them quite—
That you deemed it a pleasure, when far away,
    Long letters home to write.
      Then write them a letter to-night.

Don't think that the young and giddy friends
  Who make your pastime gay
Have half the anxious thoughts for you
  That the old folks have to-day.
For the sad old folks at home,
  With locks fast turning white,
Are longing to hear of the absent one—
  Oh, write them a letter to-night!—*Selected.*

Dear Young People.—I hope you will remember
the above poem. Girls as well as boys often forget
the dear home folks. This is very unkind. Parents
should get a good, long letter once a week—not a little hasty scribbled note. No matter if mother and
father do not answer. Your fingers are young and
nimble, theirs are old and stiff. Perhaps they *cannot*
write themselves, and it may be hard to get other
people to write.

In my many visits in the homes of the poor colored
people of the South, I have often read letters from
absent sons and daughters and written the answer.
How those dear old faces shown with pride and joy as
they exclaimed, "That is my Tom, he was always a
good boy; he never forgets his father and mother,"
and then they would ask me to read the letter over
again. If Tom and Mary could only realize how their
letters gladden the dear old folks at home, they would
put more words of love and gratitude in their letters,
and tell all the little things about their work or their
worship or their friends. Letters can't reach father
and mother after they move to heaven, and then what
a comfort it will be to your lonely heart to remember,
"I was always kind to my parents, I wrote them a
loving letter every week and put a little bit of money
into every letter, or some little gift as often as I was

able." These weekly letters will do much towards keeping you out of bad company.

Writing letters a great means of education.

Dear young people, do try and have some good, intelligent person as a correspondent, and strive yourself to write a sensible letter. I will mention a few of the many ways in which these letters will improve you. 1st. You will make a good penman, if you are careful and try to make each letter better than the former. 2nd. It will teach you how to spell correctly and write grammatically, if you examine your grammar and dictionary when in doubt about what is right. 3rd. It will give you food for thought and lead you to read and study so as to answer your correspondent. 4th. It will teach you how to express your thoughts. You think much that you cannot tell plainly, but practice in writing will improve you greatly along this line. If you stop to think you will remember many other ways in which writing letters will improve. But remember it will all depend upon the care and thought that you give to these letters.

Love Letters.

Be *careful* what you write about love affairs. If there be *real love* then every word is treasured more than gold, and every thought you express studied with the greatest of care, because your lover is trying through your letters to understand your character and feelings. Do not be extravagant in your expressions of love. Hearts filled with *true love* understand each other without so much gush and demonstration, either by letter or tongue. O be *truthful* in your letters. Most love letters are too sweet to be wholesome. Re-

fer to what pleased you in your lover's letter and say
kind things in a *sensible* way.   Do not pour out *all*
the love you feel; study self=control.   Some day you
may be ashamed of your love letters; you cannot tell
who may read them.

A Good Recommendation.

John was fifteen, and wanted a desirable place in
the office of some well known lawyer, who had ad-
vertized for a boy, but doubted his success because,
being a stranger in the city, he had no reference.

"I am afraid I will stand a poor chance," he
thought, "but I'll try and appear as well as I can,
for that may help."

So he was careful to have his dress and person
neat and when he took his turn to be interviewed,
went in with his hat in his hand, and a smile on his
face.

The keen eyed lawyer glanced him over from head
to foot.

"A good face," he thought, "and pleasant ways."

Then he noted the new suit,—but other boys had
appeared in new clothes—saw the well brushed hair
and clean looking skin.   Very well, but there had
been others here quite as cleanly; another glance
showed the finger nails free from soil.

"Ah! that looks like thoroughness," thought the
lawyer.

Then he asked a few direct, rapid questions, which
John answered as directly.

"Prompt," was the lawyer's thought; "he can
speak up when necessary.   Let me see your writing,"
he added aloud.

John took the pen and wrote his name.

"Very well, easy to read, and no flourishes. Now, what references have you?"

The dreaded question at last.

John's face fell. He began to feel some hope of success, but this dashed it.

"I have not any," he said slowly; "I'm almost a stranger in the city."

"Can't take a boy without references," was the brusque rejoinder, and as he spoke a sudden thought sent a flush to John's cheek.

"I have not references," he said with hesitation, "but here is a letter from mother I just received."

The lawyer took it. It was a short letter.

My dear John: I want to remind you that whenever you get work you must consider that work your own. Don't go into it, as some boys do, with the feeling that you will do as little as you can, and get something better soon; but make up your mind you will do as much as possible, and make yourself so necessary to your employer that he will never let you go.

You have been a good son to me. Be as good in business, and I am sure God will bless your efforts.

"H'm!" said the lawyer, reading it over a second time. "That is pretty good advice, John—excellent advice! I rather think I'll try you, even without references."

John has been with him six years, and last spring was admitted to the bar.

"Do you intend to take that young man into partnership?" asked a friend, lately.

"Yes, I do; I couldn't get along without John."

And John always says the best reference he ever

had was a mother's good advice and honest praise.—
Selected.

I want to emphasize the advice this mother gave
her son, " Whenever you get work to do, you must
consider *that work your own,* and do it so well that
your employer will feel that he can't get along without you." Persons who will slight their work when
a servant, would never do their *own* work well, and
therefore will never amount to much in any position.
A servant who does his work as " unto the Lord, and
not unto man," Col. 3: 23, will feel as great an interest as regards the prosperity of *everything* about the
house or farm as if it were their own property. O
young people, I do pray that you may all see that this
is the road to success.

Suppose that the one that employs you is unkind
and unjust, then you ask what shall I do? Do? Why
be just as faithful and as true as if you had the best
master in the world; only get another place as soon
as possible; but while there do your work faithfully.
If you slight one little task assigned to your hands,
it will leave a blot on your character and weaken
your moral nature. Read Luke 19: 17. " Thou good
servant." Why was he good? " Because thou hast
been faithful in a very little." Notice, not only a little but " a *very* little." It was the faithfulness in the
very little things that made his Lord say, " Have authority over ten cities."

To Be a Good Servant is a Great Honor.

Many persons object to being servants. This is
very foolish; everybody serves some one. If they

are of any use in the world they *are servants*. The
pastor of a church is called a minister or servant of
the church. Jesus said he was here as a servant.
"Whosoever will be chief among you let him be your
servant. Even as the Son of Man came not to be
ministered unto but to minister (to serve) and to give
his life a ransom for many." Matt. 20: 24-28. People are great in proportion to their usefulness. A
servant can add as much to the happiness of a home
as any member of the family and they are in a position to do great good or to make the whole household unhappy. No one is fit to rule till they have
learned to *serve*. Moses was brought up in luxury
and was not prepared to be a leader or a ruler till he
was trained as a servant. He was too hasty, not patient, not wise enough. Ex. 2: 12. Therefore God
made him a servant for forty years. Those who do
their part well as a servant are being prepared for
higher service. As we said a good servant has a
great influence over all the household. You have
heard the story of Georgia, the little servant girl,
who was so careful to scour the knives well and
gave as a reason, "We must shine, you in your small
corner, I in mine. This knife is in my corner and it
must shine," and through her faithful service *every*
member of the family was led to do their work better. You have also read of the little Jewish servant
girl in 1st Kings, fifth chapter, who had such an influence that on the strength of her word her master
took a long journey to see Elisha and was cured.

Titus 2: 9, 10 has rules for servants "Not answering,
not arguing," but trying to do as the one that employs you requires. Try your best to please. "Pur-

loining" means stealing slyly. This a servant is often tempted to do, because things are often left in their care, but oh, I do beseech you "show fidelity" or faithfulness in this respect, and thereby you "adorn or beautify the doctrine of God," you have a great opportunity to glorify God in the capacity of a servant. Col. 3: 22–25 shows the great reward you will get for doing your work well in order to please the Lord. Eph. 6: 5–8 gives nearly the same advice. Dearly beloved, let us be faithful in the place where God has placed us. 1st Cor. 12 shows us that we are all one in Christ, and are all needed each in his special office. In building a house the man who carries the mortar and lays the brick deserves as much honor as the architect who planned the building, provided he does it to the very best of his ability.

"Honor and fame from no condition rise,
Act well your part, there all the honor lies."

"May God help those of us who are servants not to be eye servants as men pleasers, but as the servants of Christ doing the will of God from the heart." Eph. 6: 6.

A Mother's Good-By.

Sit down by the side of your mother, my boy,
You have only a moment, I know;
But you will stay till I give you my parting advice,
It is all that I have to bestow.
You leave us to seek for employment, my boy;
By the world you have yet to be tried;
But in all temptations and struggles you meet
May your heart in the Savior confide.

You will find in your satchel a Bible, my boy;
  It is the book of all others the best;
It will teach you to live, it will help you to die,
  And lead to the gates of the blest.
I gave you to God in your cradle, my boy;
  I have taught you the best that I knew,
And as long as His mercies permit me to live
  I will never cease praying for you.

Your father is coming to wish you good=by;
  O how sad and how lone we will be!
But when far from the scenes of your childhood and
    youth
  You will remember your father and me.
I want you to heed every word I have said;
  For it comes from a heart filled with love;
And, my boy, if we never behold you on earth,
  Will you promise to meet us above?

Hold fast to the right, hold fast to the right,
  Wherever your footsteps may roam;
O forsake not the way of salvation, my boy,
  That you learned from your mother at home.
                                    —*Our Visitor.*

Honor Your Parents.

"Honor thy father and thy mother that thy days
may be long upon the land which the Lord thy God
giveth thee."—Ex. 20: 12. This commandment is
repeated away over in Eph. 6: 2, 3, where is added,
"This is the *first* commandment with promise."
Yes, it is the *only* commandment with promise.
Read the other nine and see if it be so. Notice carefully the promise, "that thy days may be long"—live
long, not in heaven, but here on earth. In Ephesians
is also added, "That it may be well with thee." Put-

ting the two promises together, they mean that you will live long and have a good time while you live. Now, my dear young friends, is not *this the very thing you want?* "O I want to have a good time," is an expression young people often use. Now here is *God's* way of getting a good time. Honor your parents, respect them, obey them, love them. Never say rude, grumbling words to father or mother. Try to make them happy. Never give them a moment's pain nor uneasiness lest you are in bad company when you are out of their sight. O my dear boy, my dear girl, be a real comfort to your parents and God's blessing will rest upon you. I know how natural it is for the young to be restless and anxious to get off where they can do as they please, when "do as I please" means running into danger and getting hurt. Like a young man I once knew who said to his mother: "I am no baby; I am a young man eighteen years old; I know how to take care of myself; let me go to the park with the other young people to-day." It was the Sabbath, and the mother feared and urged him *not* to go, but go he would. Some of the crowd got into a drunken row and our boy was arrested with the company, not because he was drunk, but because he was with drunkards. There is a verse in the Bible which reads: "He that walketh with the wise shall be wise, but a companion of fools shall be destroyed."—Prov. 13: 20. You need not be a fool, only be found in company with fools and you will be destroyed. But is it a *wise* thing to be in company with fools, or with Sabbath breakers or drunkards? O do keep out of bad company! Disobedience means in a child: "I know better than my parents; I am young, they are old; yet I know what is right better than they do. They have passed over this road it is true, and know where Satan's traps are. I have had no experience, yet I will do as I please." Is this honoring your parents? It may be true that your parents do not have as much book knowledge as you have, and yet their experience with the world has taught them the safest road to travel. If you want to have a *good time* listen to the advice of father and mother, except they tell you to do what you know is a sin against God.

Honor means respect and kindness. I know some girls who are almost ashamed of the dear old mother, who has to cook in the kitchen like a servant because her lazy daughter wants to sit in the parlor. She ought at least to help with the work till it is done, and then comb dear mother's hair and arrange her dress in a suitable manner, and then kindly lead her into the parlor and say to her young friends, " This is my dearly beloved mother," and give her the easy chair and listen to what she has to say. Let every one see that she respects and loves her mother, and do just the same with dear father. I tell you truly that if your young friends have a thimbleful of good sense then they will say, " What a sweet young lady; see how she honors her parents." And they will love you all the more for it. I have known girls to dress in the height of fashion while their mother looked as shabby as an old beggar. If I were hunting for a husband and had a beau I would notice very carefully what he said about father and mother.

Did you ever know parents to work hard to educate their children and then these same children act as if

they were ashamed of the dear parents who had sacri-
ficed so much to help them? Shame on such boys and
girls! Your education is a sham if it does not teach
you to honor and obey your parents. When President Garfield was inaugurated President of the United
States he had his aged mother by his side, anxious to
have her share his honor. I like to see a young man
lead his aged mother to church and give her a seat
and sit beside her with all the politeness he could
show to the young lady he admired. Nothing brings
the tears of joy to my eyes quicker than the tender,
loving care of a young man for his mother. I want
to take his hand and thank him.

Which Will You Have, Joy or Fun?

Perhaps you think this a strange question for Sister
Moore to ask us. What does it mean? It means
this: Many young people are wild for fun. They
will pay money, and stay up late at night, and go
with company that is not very choice, all because
they "want to have some fun," some foolish talk that
will make them laugh. If father says, "That is a
dangerous place, you had better not go, my son," then
the son replies: "Oh, father, you know young people
must have some fun." When mother says, "Daughter, I do not like that young man, the girl answers:
"Oh, mother, he is so funny, he keeps me laughing
all the time." To be able to make people laugh is a
wonderful gift. We turn aside from good, sensible
company and follow the one that can tell jokes and
keep you laughing. Eccl. 7:6 says: "The laughter
of a fool is like the crackling of thorns under a pot."

They make a great noise, but there is not substance enough in them to make the pot boil.

Now, dear children, we want you to be happy; yes, run over with joy and gladness, but not fun. We think so much fun and nonsense does not pay. When it is past it leaves you sad and restless. If something really funny happens laugh, if it be the right time to laugh, and laugh right heartily, but do not go out of your way to get fun or to make fun. Of course, joy is for the Christian. The unconverted can know nothing of it, because it is the fruit of the Spirit. Gal. 5:22. The fruit of the Spirit is love, joy, etc. Joy comes next to love. I hope you will meditate upon this lesson and quit spending so much time in giggling and nonsense, and hunting for fun, *fun*, and instead take time to read good books and write letters. Be good and do good, and your faces will shine like the morning, and your soul will sing a glad song all day long. Now, we will let sinners have the *fun* and we will have the *joy*.

Fun is Satan's substitute for joy. Fun belongs to the earth, joy is from heaven. God has planned to supply all that His children need, food for the hungry, drink for the thirsty, rest for the weary, and a pure stream of joy for those who want enjoyment. God says in John 15:11, "These things have I spoken unto you that my joy might remain in you, and that your joy might be full." *Full of joy!* Yes, God wants His children to rejoice and be glad all the days. Dear young people, if you will only ask God in faith He will put into your heart a fountain of joy that will grow purer and sweeter to the end of life.

"The joy of the Lord is the strength of his people,
The sunshine that scatters their sadness and gloom."

Let us study the following *Bible lessons:* Command to rejoice when persecuted, Matt. 5:12. The disciples *did obey* this command. Acts 5:41. Acts 13:52. Good results of trouble or persecution. James 1:2–3, 1st Pet. 4:13–16, Rom. 5:11. Joy in poverty and self-denial. 2nd Cor. 8:2 and 6:10. Joy when we suffer the loss of money or property *for Christ's sake.* Heb. 11:13. Where the joy comes from. Phil. 4:4, Rom. 15:13; 14:17. *In the Lord,* Christ's joy in us. John 17:13. Our joy then *full.* John 16:24. *Christ's joy* was to save sinners. Heb. 12:2. Our greatest joy comes from working *with Christ* to save sinners. I hope the young people will take time to study this Bible lesson.

Use What is in Your Hand for God.

Many persons say to me, "I can't do any good to any one. I don't know *where* to begin or *how* to begin." Some excuse themselves because they are not educated; others because they have so much work to do. Now the way to do good is to *do it.* Do it right where you stand this minute. Use what you have in your hand *for God.* Use what you have in your head and heart for God. Keep always in mind, "I am using this for God; I am doing my everyday work for God; I am sweeping the floor for God; I am washing the clothes for God; I am holding the plow handle for God." Let this one grand thought be with you all the time, and a light will break in upon your soul, and you will see fifty ways in which

you can do good and help others before night.   There
will be a tenderness in your voice that will comfort
the little child, a loving look in your face that will
cheer all you meet, and you will be doing good before
you know it.   Just keep in mind this one thought,
"*My whole life is for God.*"   I do all my everyday
work to please God; I dress to please the Lord; I
take my recreation or amusement to please the Lord;
I talk to please the Lord.   I am not my own, I
belong to the Lord, and though there be but little of
me, then all the more anxious am I to use that little
for the Lord.   I remember the sad history of the
servant with the *one* talent.   Matt. 25: 24–30.

I think the following verses will help you understand this lesson:

What is in Thine HAND?

"What is in thine hand, Abel?"
"Nothing but a wee lamb, O God,
  Taken from the flock;
  I purpose offering it to Thee, a willing sacrifice."
And so he did;
And the sweet smell of that burning
Has been filling the air ever since,
And constantly going up to God,
  As a perpetual sacrifice of praise.   (Heb. 11:4.)
"What is in thine hand, Moses?"
"Nothing but a staff, O God,
  With which I tend my flock."
"Take it and use it for me," said God.
  And so he did, and with it
  Wrought more wondrous things
  Than Egypt and her proud
  King had ever done before.   (Ex. 4:2.)

"Mary, what is that thou hast in thine hand?"
"Nothing but a pot of sweet-smelling
Ointment, O God, wherewith I would
Anoint this Holy One, who is
Called Jesus." And so she did;
And not only did the perfume fill
All the house in which they were
But the whole Bible-reading world
Has been fragrant with the memory
Of that blessed act of love, which
Has ever since been spoken of
As a memorial of her.   (Mark 14:9.)
"Poor widow, what is that thou hast
In thine hand?" said God.
"Only two mites, Lord;
It is very little; but then it is all I have,
And I would put it into thy treasury."
And so she did.
And the story of her generous
Giving has ever since wrought
Like a charm, in prompting   (Luke 21:1-4.)
Others to give to the Lord.

"What is that in thine hand, Dorcas?"
"Only a needle, Lord." "Take it
And use it for me," said God.
And so she did; and not only were
The suffering poor of Joppa
Warmly clad, but inspired by
This loving life, Dorcas societies
Even now continue to ply
Their divine mission to the poor
Throughout the earth.   (Acts 9:36-43.)

My Precious Bible.

Like a star of the morning in its beauty,
　Like a sun is the Bible to my soul;
Shining clear on the way of love and duty,
　As I hasten to the City of the King.

Holy Bible!　My precious Bible!　Gift of God,
　And lamp of life.　My beautiful Bible!
I will cling to the dear old holy Bible,
　As I hasten to the City of the King.

'T is the voice of a friend forever near me,
　In the toil and the battle here below;
In the gloom of the valley it will cheer me
　Till the glory of His kingdom I shall know.

It shall stand in its beauty and its glory,
　When the earth and the heavens pass away;
Ever telling the blessed, wondrous story,
　Of the loving Lamb, the only living way.

—Selected.

BIBLE BANDS.

A Bible Band is a simple plan to get old and young, converted and unconverted to study God's word daily, yes study the Bible; not merely read it but "Search the Scriptures." Look carefully into every verse. It contains "hidden treasure," and you must search to find it. The paper HOPE is a part of the Bible Band. It contains a certain lesson for every day in each month, for the student, and a plain, practical explanation of the lesson which helps and directs his study.

Who Can Belong to the Bible Band?

Old and young, converted and unconverted should meet together in the Bible Bands. In fact they should also be together in the Sabbath school and in all the church services. God put them together in the home, which is really God's first church. The young need the advice and guidance of the old, and the old need the hope and vigor of the young. Remember we want the little children to be members of the Bible Band.

BIBLE BAND CONSTITUTION.

ARTICLE 1. Each member shall study the same *daily* lessons which are given in HOPE, and commit to memory at least one new text each week. Those who are young and quick to learn can memorize more.

ART. 2. It shall be the duty of the members to read the Bible to others, especially to the sick or those who cannot read, as often as opportunity affords.

ART. 3. It shall be the duty of the members to do all in their power to supply the destitute with Bibles, and to use their influence to get every man, woman and child to own and read the Bible.

ART. 4. It shall be the duty of the members to carry with them a Bible when they go on a visit, or to church, or any meeting. (Suggestion.) It is also a good plan to keep a little Testament in our pockets while at work, so we can read at leisure moments.

ART. 5. The members of the Band shall meet once a week to review the weekly lessons and make a report of Bible work. They are expected to answer the following questions: (1) How many days have you carefully studied the lesson? (2) How many texts have you memorized? (3) To how many persons have you read the Bible? (4) How much money given? The secretary is expected to keep the above record.

If members live too far away, or other duties prevent, they may send written reports as often as possible. Persons can belong to the Band if they cannot read, if they will promise to have some one read to them.

ART. 6. The officers of the society shall be: president, vice=president, secretary and treasurer. The duty of said officers to be the same as in any other society. The officers to be elected every six months.

Bible Band Verse.

"This book of the law shall not depart out of thy mouth, but thou shalt meditate therein day and night, that thou mayest observe to do according to all that is written therein; for then shalt thou make thy way prosperous, and then shalt thou have good success." Josh. 1:8.

Bible Band Prayer.

O God, help me to remember that thou art talking to me when I read the Bible, and may I believe every word thou sayest. May the Holy Spirit shine in my heart, and make the meaning plain; and make me willing to obey all thy commands. This I ask in Jesus' name. Amen.

Rules for Reading the Bible.

1st. Remember that God talks to you when you read the Bible. In prayer you talk to God.

2d. If I am a saved sinner, I should stop at every promise for a Christian, and ask if I believe it, and rest my soul upon it; and stop at every command, and ask if I obey it cheerfully.

3d. If I am an unsaved sinner, I should stop at every invitation of mercy, and ask my own heart why I do not accept it, and remember that God will accept no service or work at my hands till I receive the pardon for my sins that Jesus bought with His own blood. I have only to accept and believe His promise and then I am a saved sinner, and ready for work on earth and a home in heaven.

4th. I should remember that all the Bible stories and all its histories of individuals and nations have been written for my warning or for my encouragement or my learning, and I should stop as I read till I get the lesson for my own heart. 1 Cor. 10:11.

5th. I should meditate or think about what I have read in the Bible, and talk about it to others. I should commit as much as possible of it to memory. Josh. 1:8, Ps. 1:2, and Deut. 6:7.

6th. When I read the Bible I should get a dictionary and find the meaning of every word, or ask some one to explain what I do not understand. I should learn how to use a concordance and a reference Bible, and use them. Acts 8:30–33, Luke 24:27.

Young People's Societies.

These societies have done good for two reasons: First the wise and good old people who were interested met them and guided and encouraged them. Second, the young had been hindered in the active work of the church by the domineering spirit of many of the old members, but in these young people's societies the young were encouraged to use their talents no matter how awkward the effort at first, and therefore they have grown strong and helpful.

However, there is danger in the separation of the young from the old. It may lead the young to feel too independent, and not give the respect and reverence to the aged that God requires.

Had the older people been wise, and carefully trained the young to *work in the church*, prayer meeting, and Sabbath school, there would have been no *need* for any other organization. In fact, we would never have needed the Sabbath school if the church worship or the sermons had contained more Bible study. Most of the sermons of the present day teach us but little about the Bible. I carry my Bible to church, but what is the use if the preacher only gives me his text? Our Bible Bands are really a church service in which we are striving to get back to the old plan of reading and explaining the Scriptures as Jesus did in Luke 4: 16–21, also Luke 24: 25–27. Get your Bibles and read it. The apostles gave us the same kind of instruction in their sermons.

In many places the pastor is the teacher of the Bible Band, and this is right. He will never get a better chance to put the gospel down into the hearts of his people. His audience will be interested because it is a review of Bible lessons that they have been studying all the week. Bible Bands can do the same work as the Christian Endeavor.

In the Christian Endeavor and other young people's societies a pledge is taken, but it does not cover the conduct of the home life as fully as we wish. We reckon the *whole family* in our Fireside school. Yes, ours is a beautiful young people's society as well as one for mother. God put parents and children together, and what God has joined we do not want to put asunder. Especially do young and old *each need the other* in work and worship for God.

Old and Young Should Worship Together.

God's plan is to have old and young together in the public worship of God as well as around the fireside.

Old people going towards the church, the young people going from it.

You can see this every Sabbath. The streets are thronged with children hastening away from the church where they have been to Sabbath school, and their parents going to hear the sermon, while they leave their children to spend the rest of the day in another school where Satan catches away all the good seed of the morning. Now, is this wise?

Dear young people, I do beseech you stay to the morning service with your parents, and do all you can to help them get ready for the Sabbath school. Rise early and help mother with the Sunday morning work. Help her Saturday night to get ready for the Sabbath day.

Those who desire further instruction on the subject of Bible Bands please write to Joanna P. Moore, 513 Mulberry street, Nashville, Tenn.

Young People's Pledge.

Several of the young people have said to me "You have given mother a pledge to govern her daily life; we are willing to take one also," therefore we give the following:

Pledge.

"First I promise by God's help that I will lovingly obey my parents and share with them in the household care and labor for the support of the family, and help teach the younger children. If my parents have not had the opportunity of an education when young, I will take pleasure in reading to them and teaching them, and do it in a loving, respectful manner.

Second, I will try to be a good pattern for the younger children, and for all my young companions. Especially, as a sister, I will try to protect my brothers from idle and intemperate company by making *home* pleasant for them. As a brother, I will remember that my mother and sisters have the first claim on my leisure time until I become a husband.

Third, since a meek and quite spirit makes me more beautiful in God's sight than fashionable dresses, and costs no money, therefore I will take more time in adorning my heart and brain with the beauties of religion and all useful knowledge. I will strive to be of as little expense as possible to my parents.

Fourth, I promise that I will join with my parents in the daily study of the Bible and prayer, and that I will do all I can to help mother keep her pledge.

(The above pledge is just as appropriate for the children as for the young men and women.)

Be the Best You Can.

My boy, you're soon to be a man;
　Get ready for a man's work now,
And learn to do the best you can
　When sweat is brought to arm and brow.
Don't be afraid, my boy, to work:
　You've got to, if you mean to win;
He is a coward who will shirk:
　Roll up your sleeves, and then "go in!"

Don't wait for chances; look about!
　There's always something you can do,
He who will manfully strike out
　Finds labor—plenty of it, too;
But he who folds his hands and waits
　For "something to turn up" will find
The toiler passes Fortune's gates,
　While he, alas! is left behind.

Be honest as the day is long;
　Don't grind the poor man for his cent;
In helping others you grow strong,
　And kind deeds done are only lent;
And this remember; if you're wise,
　To your own business be confined;
He is a fool, and fails, who tries
　His fellow=men's affairs to mind.

Don't be discouraged and get blue
    If things don't go to suit you quite;
Work on!   Perhaps it rests with you
    To set the wrong that worries right.
Don't lean on others.   Be a man!
    Stand on a footing of your own;
Be independent if you can,
    And cultivate a sound backbone.

Be brave and steadfast, kind and true,
    With faith in God and fellow=men,
And win from them a faith in you
    By doing just the best you can.

                        —*Selected.*

God's Blessed Book.

What book ought I to love the best,
And on its truths securely rest?
    The Bible, the Bible,
    God's blessed book, the Bible.

CHORUS.

It bids my spirit cease to rove,
It tells me of my Savior's love,
And points me to my home above,
    God's blessed book, the Bible.

What tells me of my fallen state,
And how God can me anew create?
    The Bible, the Bible.
    God's blessed book, the Bible.

What points me to the Lamb of God,
To trust in his atoning blood?
    The Bible, the Bible,
    God's blessed book, the Bible.

What warns me to abstain from sin,
And tends to make me pure within?
    The Bible, the Bible.
    God's blessed book, the Bible.

NO BOOK COMPLETE WITHOUT BIBLE

LESSONS.

I tried to finish this book without giving some Bible lessons but I *could not*. Of all that I wish you to learn, the Bible is the most important. God grant that the readers of this book may take time for one month to read these lessons *daily* and thereby learn to love *daily* study.

Hope.

In our paper HOPE we have a daily lesson. Through these lessons many little children and young people as well as older ones, are learning to read God's word daily and according to a plan or system. They are learning to be as hungry for their Bible lesson as they are for their breakfast. Like Jeremiah, "They eat God's words and it is to them the joy and rejoicing of their hearts." Jer. 15: 16.

How to Read These Lessons.

Have your Bible in your hand and hunt out all the texts of Scripture referred to. We do not put them in this book because we want you to read them *directly from God's own book*. If possible take time to think and read more than simply the text quoted. Read the context or the verses before and after and you will get a fuller meaning. Be sure to hunt up in your Bible *every* text referred to.

Bible Lessons on Courtship and Marriage.

Dear Young People: You cannot finish this book without your Bibles. Do you really own a Bible? Do you love your Bible? Do you read your Bible *prayerfully every* day? I would like to know the answer to these last three questions.

Lesson for First Day of the Month.

Josh. 1:8. This is our Bible Band verse but I fear all the young people do not understand it as they should. In this verse there are *three* commands and *two* promises. 1st. "This book of the law"—which means the Bible—"shall not depart out of thy mouth." You talk with your mouth, therefore this means God's word shall form a part of all your conversation. In this way you teach others, and by the Bible you must prove to others that you are right. Isa. 8:20. Second command. Meditate or think over in your mind what you have read and pray for help to keep this law. The Bible is a good subject for quiet thought alone, and will keep bad thoughts out of your heart. Third. *Do*, DO, DO what the Bible tells you. If the *do* is left out, all your talk and thought are in vain. Now the promises are: 1st. You will prosper. 2nd. You will be a real success. This is just what all young people desire, success and prosperity. Obey these three commands and the promises are sure. *Your* life will be a success.

Second Day.

Genesis 2: 21–24. No one can read this without

feeling that marriage is the most mysterious and sacred and close relation of life. The husband and wife are "one." All their interests are the same after marriage. Now read 2 Cor. 6: 14, and tell me how can a Christian marry one who has no interest in what is to him the great object of life, namely, *to glorify God?* It is impossible to put two such persons together as true husband and wife. You simply come together on the low plane of fleshly love. None of that perfect fellowship of soul and mind that makes the strength and enjoyment of each individual *double what it was before marriage.* Oh, how we have perverted God's plan for a happy home on earth.

Third Day.

Deut. 7:3, 4. I have known many young men and women who marry into the world with the hope that they could bring their companions to Christ. God is merciful, and in a few cases they were converted; or, perhaps I ought to say, *both* were converted, because, how could you be a true Christian and marry contrary to God's command? It is true, also, that many a man and woman *pretend* to be a Christian in order to win one that is a Christian, but it seems to me that those in close touch with the Lord Jesus could detect the hypocrite before marriage. The truth is you let your affections run away with your brains and your religion both. Be calm, be thoughtful, be watchful, be prayerful. Your *marriage is the greatest event of your life,* next to your conversion.

Fourth Day.

Neh. 13:23, 24. One object of marriage is the

propagation of the human race. God intended the home to be a place where *children* would be trained for the service of God. Sons and daughters are a great blessing sent from God and you should be *prepared to receive them.* Every husband and wife should make *this part* of the marriage relation a subject of *prayer and not of lust.* Verse 24 says, these children were half heathen. The influence of one parent was for God, the other for the world. You all know how difficult it is to rear children right when the parents do not agree, and since Satan has divided God's church up into sects (1 Cor. 1:11–13) it is best to marry in the *same* denomination. Lovers should talk and pray about these subjects in a common-sense way, and thus become acquainted with each other's real character, and spend less time in kisses and other manifestations of affection, which tend to deaden the intellect and create unholy love. On this subject also read Ezra 9:10, 11, yes, all of Ezra's prayer in this chapter.

Fifth Day.

Before we leave this subject of intermarriage with unbelievers, read Judges 14:15–17; also Neh. 13:26; 1 Kings 11:1–8. In the first place, Solomon did wrong in having more than *one* wife. Read Deut. 17:17. This matter of having many wives was *not* God's plan any more than the law of divorce, but he allowed it because of the hardness of their hearts (Mark 10:2–9). Never marry with the thought in your heart that if you do not like your partner you can have a divorce. Remember, *God* joins you together (verse 9), and no law of man can put you asunder. All young people should study the Bible on these subjects *before marriage.*

Sixth Day.

Gen. 24:1-9. Abraham is called always the "Friend of God." Perhaps he was the most faithful and holy of the Old Testament saints. You see how anxious he was about the marriage of his son Isaac. I do not know the relation of this servant to whom he gave this solemn charge, but he controlled all Abraham possessed (verse 2). Notice (verse 7) God sent an "angel before this servant." I like to think that to-day God sends an angel to every young woman in answer to prayer and makes her willing to go with her "Isaac" when he calls her. There is no doubt about it, God does guide about marriage when we will let Him do it. All parents do not look upon marriage with the reverence Abraham felt. Right here we venture a word of warning to parents, teachers and all who have the care of the young.

One of the Greatest Sins of the Age.

When we joke or tease our young people about love between the sexes, we take away from this holiest of all earthly affections its sacredness and truthfulness. They think this love is only a joke, and so they begin to flirt and deceive one another, and they will tell lies to every one about it. A boy will say solemnly, He don't care a fig for the girl he loves devotedly, and *vice versa.* They *are driven to this* by the way you tease them. Even when they are but little children

we begin to joke them about their "girl" or their
"beau." Parents, friends, I beseech you never make
fun of your children when you notice in them a growing love for one of the opposite sex. *Encourage them
to confide in you.* Tell them quietly that it is God's
plan that they should thus love some one, that it is
nothing to be ashamed of, but, if kept under perfect
control, it is the purest and sweetest affection of life.
Do not let the other children make fun of them
I would rather joke about my mother's death than
about that God-given love that should be in every
" Rebecca's " heart for her " Isaac," and *vice versa.*

Seventh Day.

Gen. 24: 54–58. Parents in those days had much
to do with the selection of companions for their children. We would advise the young people of to-day
to pay more attention to the advice of father and
mother on this subject of courtship and marriage.
They are your *best* friends; confide in them. And
yet they must not assume too much control. You
notice in verses 57 and 58 they would not send Rebecca away until they had *asked her consent.* This
is a beautiful love story. Boys and girls, read the
whole chapter. It will do you good to read such a
calm, common-sense love story as this.

Gen. 24: 61–67. I do not know how far Isaac came
to meet his bride, but I know what he was accustomed
to do while the servant was away getting his wife,
and that was *pray.* In verse 63 "meditate" means
pray. Indeed, you know that quiet meditation or
thought without the lips moving, is often the deepest

prayer. Dear young people, you need more of this *holy, not unholy*, meditation, so that you may meet your lover in the right spirit. Notice verse 67. It means so much. Isaac *loved* Rebecca and Rebecca *comforted* Isaac. The dear mother who loved Isaac so devotedly was dead, and now the wife seems to fill the place of mother as well as wife. How beautiful!

Eighth Day.

Gen. 26: 34, 35; also Gen. 27: 46. You see what trouble the marriage with those of another religion brought to this home. I fear Esau did not ask the advice of his parents about marriage. In Gen. 28: 1–5 you see how important this subject seemed in the eyes of Isaac and Rebecca. Every good parent feels the same solicitude about their children's marriage, therefore I want the children to confide and counsel with father and mother about it. Do not be head-strong, but listen to the advice of *good* friends.

Ninth Day.

Gen. 34: 1. This is such a sad history that I do not like to call attention to it. But I must "hoist the danger signal," because thousands of young girls are going the way Dinah went. Mother "Leah" dresses them up and sends them out to see the "daughters of the land"—the fashions of the world. What right had mother to send out that sweet young girl unprotected? She might have known some evil would befall her. I knew a mother who would send her daughter off on an excursion, much against my advice, and she returned ruined for life.   Did I say I knew *one?*   Yes, I can safely say I know *hundreds* who **thus** expose both sons and daughters to perilous temptations, because it is the fashion to attend parks, parties, worldly amusements, etc.   My dear daughters, if you have a sensible mother who *forbids* you to go with worldly fashionable people, then be wise and obey her wishes.   See what trouble Dinah brought upon the whole family.   She led her brothers into fearful sin and nearly broke her father's heart.   V. 30.

Adultery, sinful lust, in some form or other, is a highway by which many of our young people go down to destruction.   A desire to gad abroad so as to show fine dress, is a great temptation to many girls.   O God, give us quiet, modest young women who *love to stay at home* and grow to be strong women by their mothers' fireside!

DUTIES OF HUSBAND AND WIFE.

Tenth Day.

A wise man or woman studies carefully the conditions of an engagement before they agree. If you are to teach a school or hire out for any service you say, "What do you expect of me? What am I to expect of you?" But our silly young people engage to be husband and wife without even asking, "What is required of me? Am I prepared for this important relation?" Is it any wonder that misunderstandings, domestic quarrels and divorces should follow such foolish marriages? Let us examine a few texts in our law book. Titus 2: 4. Wife, this is for you. Be sober, give up your foolish, giddy ways. *No flirting after marriage,* nor before it either. Be a quiet, sensible woman and *love* your husband and children. No matter if they do not respect you. It is *your* duty to *love.* Just here is perhaps the place to mention the sad fact, that many *married* men are flirts. They are exposed to more temptations than the wife, being so much away from home. They *sometimes pass for single men.* I am afraid of the faithfulness of a married man with whom I have spent ten minutes in conversation and have not heard *one word about his dear wife.* Our best young girls often write to me of the way young girls are led astray by married men. Alas! alas! that such things should be.

Eleventh Day.

Titus 2: 5. Five duties in this one verse. Discreet means wise. Shun the appearance of evil. I called at 8 p. m. on a young wife. Her husband's business kept him out till 9. I found in her room a young man. I believe they were both good and pure, but this was not "discreet." Keep young men and *old* men too away from your home as much as possible while your husband is absent. This is one way to prove that you are "chaste," which means pure in morals. "Good housekeeper." Every husband loves a nice, clean, orderly home. This will require industry. Notice Prov. 31: 11–16.

Twelfth Day.

Col. 3: 18; Eph. 5: 22; Tit. 2: 5;1 Pet. 3: 1. "Wives obey." Yes, *obey.* It is all through the Bible. Therefore, be careful that you choose a husband that you *can reverence and obey.* If you do not obey there will be no order or discipline in your home. *It is God's plan*, and very foolish in you to rebel. It is true you are to obey "as is fit in the Lord," etc. (Col. 3:18). But about the general management of the house; etc., you are the one must yield, unless what the husband wants you to do is *a real sin* against God. I knew a couple who had a very serious quarrel about the arrangement of the furniture. I told the wife that if her husband wanted the dressing bureau to stand in the middle of the dining-room, I would let it stand there rather than quarrel. Of course it was scarcely *his right* to interfere about

those little home affairs, but, wife, you are the one to
yield, unless there is sin in the command

Thirteenth Day.

Come here, young man. Get your Bible and find
1 Pet. 3: 7. You heard what I said to that young
woman who is to be your wife about obeying. All
right, but you must have " knowledge," wisdom, so
as to know how to command. One at the head needs
to *know more* than the one that obeys. Give " honor,"
respect to your wife. The best chair, the choicest
piece of beefsteak at the breakfast table, etc. She
is not as strong as you are physically, so do not give
her the *heaviest* burden to carry, while you sit in
your easy chair. I saw a husband and wife walking
together. He was flourishing a little cane in his
hand, she carrying in her arms a heavy baby.

Fourteenth Day.

Eph. 5: 25–33. Notice what wonderful devotion,
what love, what tenderness is required of the husband. Surely *any* woman might gladly agree to
obey one who loved thus. No hard command would
be given where such love existed. My dear young
people, God has planned it all right. If you will just
follow the Bible laws of marriage you will have a
happy married life. But, dearly beloved young
people, be sure that you have found the woman you
can thus love and cherish. Young woman, pray
much to know if this is the man you can safely follow
and lovingly obey. I have only given you a few

texts. You must take your Bible and together search for others.

Fifteenth Day.

Beloved friends, I have spent much of my long life in carrying the gospel into the homes of the people. Nothing has discouraged me as much as the angry words and harsh rebukes of the men and women who, before the marriage altar, promised "to love and cherish till death do us part." It is so hard after the *first* quarrel to bring husband and wife together. I am terribly afraid of the *first* quarrel. Much of this trouble is the result of ignorance as respects the duties of the marriage relation. *No common sense person wants to make his or her home a place of torment rather than a place of comfort and rest.* We will give you Eph. 4: 31, 32, because I fear some who read this book may have had their first quarrel, and this is the way to be friends again.

Sixteenth Day.

I think of another lesson on this subject. It is Col. 3: 18, 19. "Wives submit" or obey, but not blindly, but see if each command is "fit in the Lord" or *right* before you obey. Husband, if you are at the head be not bitter, but be *tender* and *patient with your wife,* which you will be if you love her devotedly, therefore you are told to "*love* your wife." *Those who command need more love than those who obey.* Eph. 5: 25, tells the husband to love the wife as Christ loves His church, which, of course, is a *greater love* than the church has for Christ. This pure, uuselfish love of the husband should make the wife very thoughtful and anxious to please her husband, and give the reverence required in Eph. 5: 33.

Seventeenth Day.

Prov. 22: 6. It is utterly impossible to train a child properly in a home where the husband and wife do not treat each other with love and respect. If your boy sees you selfish and overbearing with your wife he will be likely to treat his wife the same way when he gets one. He will do it without thinking, because *home example is such a powerful teacher.* I heard a young wife say: " My mother never obeyed father. She did as she pleased, and I can't submit to these things." And soon this home was as unhappy as her mother's had been. O beloved, for the sake of your children make your home a pure and happy place—a beautiful, sweet pattern by which they can model their earthly nests when they have flown from yours.

Eighteenth Day.

Did you ever hear of the man who said, "We have two ' bears' in our home, and by their presence we keep things in peace and order?" You will find one of these bears in Eph. 4: 2. Forbearing here means to keep from being cross when you are treated unkindly, and you do it " in love." But in order to do so you must have two of the "fruits of the Spirit "— meekness and long-suffering. Notice the verse carefully; also verse 3. "Unity," oneness of the Spirit "in the bond of peace." Unless there is peace around the fireside it will be impossible to train your children rightly. *Nothing can be taught in confusion.* In every home trying accidents will happen, and some member of the family, in an unguarded moment, will be impatient, therefore you need the "forbear."

Nineteenth Day.

Here is the other "bear" in Gal. 6: 2. *To carry a burden for others lightens our own.* It is such a joy to forget one's self and "lend a hand" to one in need. "Mother is tired. Daughter, you go and get dinner." "That washing is too hard for Mary. Hang out the clothes for her." "Little Tommy can't make his kite fly. Sister, lay down your book and go and show him." "John, do please try and rise early and make the fire for mother." "Father, do try and stay at home to-night. Mother is so lonesome when you are away." O there are so many ways to lighten burdens and cheer hearts if we are willing and watchful. Remember it is the "law of Christ" to bear one another's burdens. *To be helped does not make us half as happy as helping others,* because Acts 20: 35.

Twentieth Day.

Now since the "bears" have brought peace to our home, we will talk a little more about the children. Ex. 20:5, gives this solemn warning: "I am a jealous God, visiting the iniquities of the fathers upon the children unto the third and fourth generation of them that hate me." You all know that a child inherits a love for strong drink from drunken parents. The bad temper, the tendency to adultery, etc., are all transmitted in the same way to the poor child. O parents, I beseech you for the sake of your children live pure, holy lives, before your children are born. Some one asked, "How early in life should you begin to train a child?" The answer was, "Fifty years before the child was born," meaning by this that the good training of parents and grandparents helped to train the child, because the children inherit the character of the parents, be it good or bad. How sad that a child should come unto life with a bend in the wrong direction.

Twenty-first Day.

Gal. 6:7, 8. Young people often think that they can indulge in wicked habits and live a fast life till they marry, and then settle down. But alas, those evil habits cling to them. If God gives them children they, too, will suffer. Many a young man and woman too, is a perfect wreck at twenty, and not prepared either physically or mentally for the holy duties of parentage. From a child you should live a temperate, pure life and do all in your power to have a healthy body. Girls, take off your corsets and give your vital organs *room to grow*. Boys, throw away your liquor and tobacco and grow up to be strong, healthy men.

Twenty-second Day.

Luke 1:6. Husband and wife "righteous before

God, walking in all the commandments of God blame-
less." What a happy home that must have been, and
yet, *no home fills its mission perfectly without children.* Therefore, they both prayed for a child. Verse
13 proves that Zacharias had prayed thus. I am
always sorry when I hear good men and women say,
"Thank God, I have no children." If they are wicked
and profligate, I too, am glad if they are childless.
This child of prayer, John the Baptist, was a consecrated, holy child, *like his parents.*

Twenty-third Day.

All children should be given in answer to prayer,
consecrated to the Lord before they are born. I want
you to stop and think about the character of some
children who came in answer to earnest prayer.
Isaac, Joseph, Samuel, John the Baptist. Get your
Bible and read the history of these men of God.
They are the holiest and best men the Bible tells us
of. Alas, for the children that are *begotten in lust*
without a prayer or a thought of God. Parents, I
leave this subject for your meditation. Young people, think of this evil before you become husband and
wife, so as to avoid it.

OTHER LESSONS FOR THE YOUNG.

Twenty-fourth Day.

Gen. 39: 9. Read this whole chapter; notice verse 2. God was with Joseph and made him prosperous. Getting into prison only *helped* to make Joseph great, because he was there for conscience sake. Surely never was a young man more severely tempted than was Joseph, but he was like Paul, he "had his body under control." O that every young person, when tempted to commit adultery might say with Joseph, "How can I do this great wickedness and sin against God?" Joseph was *afraid of sin*. There are many women to-day like Potiphar's wife who are laying traps to catch our good, pure young men. God help them to remember Joseph and die rather than sin against God. Proverbs 7th chapter, describes these bad women. Read it and take warning, young men.

Twenty-fifth Day.

Dan. 1: 1–8. Here are four young men away from home among ungodly people, and yet mark you, how strong and courageous they were. Daniel led and the others followed. "Purposed in his heart." Made a strong resolution that he would not drink the wine nor eat the meat that was offered to idols. This is what we mean by a temperance pledge. He made

this resolution when he knew the king had power to
kill him if he did not obey.   What shall I say to those
poor, weak young men who will drink wine, beer,
toddy, etc., rather than bear a taunt on account of
their temperance principles?   Some who are taught
temperance when at home become weak when exposed to temptation.   Young men, I beseech you:

> "Dare to be a Daniel,
>   Dare to stand alone,
>   Dare to have a purpose firm,
>   Dare to *make it known.*"

Twenty-sixth Day.

Dan. 1: 7–21., Read the whole chapter. Plain food,
such as these young men ate, made them healthier
(v. 12–15) than those who ate meat and drank wine.
Verse 20 tells us, their minds were clearer than those
of the other students.   They were *ten times smarter*
and more intelligent.   We know that their souls were
purer; so we may safely conclude that temperance is
good for the body, good for the mind, and *good for the
soul.*   I am sure you must admire the character of
Joseph and Daniel and his three friends.   Remember
you can do right, no matter if you are surrounded by
the very devils of hell; God is stronger than all your
enemies put together.   Read 2 Chronicles 32: 7, 8,
and Phil. 4: 13.

Twenty-seventh Day.

1 Chronicles 28: 9, 10.   Here is another young man
starting out on his life's work and this was his father's

advice to him. Notice verse 8; he was to search for all the commandments. Verse 9 says he must have a right heart and a willing mind. Why? Because God sees both. Notice the warning at the last of this verse. *You* also have a great house to build; you yourself are the "sanctuary," the house that God lives in. Now see to it that you do all you can to make your *body healthy and strong,* and your mind and heart and character the same. Besides this, the work you have to do in life is just as important for *you* as Solomon's was for himself. Perhaps your father or mother gave you the same advice and warning that David did his son. Have you wandered away and forgotten the advice?

Read 1 Kings 3: 3–14. Vs. 8, 9.—Solomon you see *began* right. He has offered a sacrifice to show that all he has belongs to God, and now he prays a wise prayer and Solomon was all that God said he would be; but notice the *warning* in verse 14. Alas! even Solomon did not heed this warning.

Twenty-eighth Day.

1 Kings 11: 1–8, also Neh. 13: 26. I do not like to teach this lesson but I must, as a warning. You see how high we may be and yet fall into sin, and fall through the sin of adultery. Alas! how many are being led astray by this terrible vice. Solomon began when quite young to disobey God along this line, and kept on till he was old. Deut. 17: 17. O how sad! Young men and old men, beware of this sin that ruined even as great a man as Solomon. "Let him that thinketh he standeth take heed lest he fall."

Keep away from "strange women." Be faithful to your *one* wife; many wives or many lovers are dangerous. No wonder Paul said, " I keep under my body and bring it into subjection, lest after having preached to others, I myself should be a castaway." 1 Cor. 9: 24–27. You can see the difference between Paul and Solomon. One controlled his lusts, the other gratified them. Take warning, young people, before it is too late.

Twenty-ninth Day.

Psalm 119: 9. In this verse a question is asked and the answer is also given. A very important question. How shall a young man cleanse his way? Every young man wants a clean way, a clean heart, a clean record. He wants to be able to say: "My name has never been mentioned in connection with unjust or dishonorable conduct; I have traveled a clean road, I have kept out of bad company, I have the good name which is worth more than riches." Prov. 22:1. I am sure this is the longing desire of all who are just starting out in life. Notice the answer: "Take heed hereto according to thy word." The Bible points to the narrow but the safe road. Take heed and be careful that you follow the advice given in God's word, or you are a lost young man, a lost young woman.

Psalm 19:10, 11. Happy and safe is the young man or woman who can say with all his heart these two short verses. First he has "sought the Lord with his whole heart." God has said elsewhere in his word, "Thou shalt find me in the days that thou seekest me with thy whole heart." Therefore through this prayer he finds the Lord, and now the young man prays, "O let me not wander from thy commandments."

Thirtieth Day.

Mark 10: 21, 22. Study carefully the two verses if you cannot memorize them, and find the same narrative in Matthew and Luke, and study it altogether. I know a great many such young men. They are good and kind to their parents, pleasant companions, upright in their dealings, etc., but *one thing they lack*. They do not love the Lord Jesus. They have not taken up the cross. They do not follow the meek and lowly Savior. They have some idol hidden away in their hearts, something that they love more than they do Jesus. In this case it was *money*. Sometimes it is worldly pleasure, or fashion, or folly of some kind. But, dear young man, remember that this verse says, "Jesus loved him," and he also loves *you*. Strange that Jesus' tender love for you does not break your hard heart and lead you to repentance.

Many mothers say to me, "My boy or girl is good to me, they obey me and work for me, but alas! they are not Christians." They are like the young man in our lesson. This "*one* thing that they lack" will shut them out of heaven and away forever from their dear mother. Young people, do you all follow Jesus? It *will pay* in time and eternity. Read Mark 8: 36, 37, 38. Christ is the *only* door into heaven; your good moral character will not save you. Jesus is the only Savior.

Thirty-first Day.

Acts 12:13, 14. I like to think of this young
woman who attended the all day and all night prayer
meeting for Peter while he was in prison. I do not
know whether she was a servant that went to answer
the door bell for the family, or perhaps she was
Mary's daughter. It matters not. She belonged to
the "household of faith," where there is no "respect
of persons." She knew Peter; she followed with
God's people; she was greatly interested in the work
of the church. This we know. I like to think of
her sweet young face there at that prayer meeting
with the older ones. I like the plan of old and
young, and the little babies in their mothers' arms,
all coming together to the church of God. Our way
of putting the children together in the Sunday school
and the young people in their societies, I fear is not
God's plan. May all the young "Rhodas" come and
worship with their fathers and mothers. It is the
safest way. It is God's way.

Joanna Patterson Moore (Sept. 26, 1832-April 15, 1916) has long been recognized as a missionary hero of the American Baptists. But few realize that she had a sanctification experience in a Methodist Camp meeting that propelled her into ministry, an experience she freely spoke and wrote about. She grew up and trained as a teacher in Pennsylvania, till a dramatic vision compelled her to go to Island Number Ten in 1863, little more than a sandbar in the Mississippi River where the Northern Army as was holding African-American slaves as confiscated property. There she worked among 1,000 African-American freed slaves who lived in complete destitution.

Following the Civil War, Moore continued to feel called to serve African-Americans in need, and so she worked in Louisiana, Arkansas, and Mississippi and became known as the "Swamp Angel of the South." She cared for elderly freed slaves who had no one to care for them, and she expanded her ministry to include an education effort to help African-American women called the Fireside Schools. With a Christian literacy magazine called Hope, she taught the bible and basic literacy to thousands of African-American women in their homes.

It was through the Fireside Schools and the magazine Hope, that Joanna Moore introduced the experience of sanctification to African-American women, including Mother Lizzie Robinson, who was appointed by Charles Mason in 1912 as the General Overseer of the Women's Work of the Church of God in Christ (COGIC), currently the fifth largest denomination in the United States and one of the best known Pentecostal-Holiness churches in the African-American community.

Moore was the first white woman missionary appointed by the American Baptist Home Missionary Society to work among African-American communities in the South during Reconstruction. When she died in 1916 in Nashville, Tennessee, she was buried at her request in an African-American cemetery.

www.ingramcontent.com/pod-product-compliance
Lightning Source LLC
Chambersburg PA
CBHW021154020426
42331CB00003B/56